TRIPPIN' AND SIPPIN'

TRIPPIN' AND SIPPIN'

A QUEST FOR BOMB VINHO

ADAM LOVELL

parea BOOKS

EDITOR'S NOTE

I moved to Lisbon in June 2022, after having only decided in April that I'd leave Los Angeles and start a new life in Europe. Trusting only a fifteen-minute video call with a broker recommended by a friend, I signed the lease on my apartment in Alfama from across the Atlantic. That first night, as I rode in an Uber from the airport to my new home, I got a text message from a friend: would I meet up with two of her friends who were also in Lisbon? And could I recommend a good spot for a glass of wine? Of course I couldn't; I hadn't even stepped foot in my apartment, but at that moment the car drove by a buzzy yet understated-looking restaurant called SEM. I looked it up, saw 4.9 stars on Google, and without hesitating, recommended it as our meeting place for the evening.

The three of us sat down at a table outside, Adam appearing not long after. He asked us a couple of questions about what kind of wine we liked, but it was clear he had his favorites that he wanted us to try. We each ordered a different wine, keen to taste a handful of options, and I specifically remember thinking, "This is the best glass of wine I've had in a while. Imagine what people in New York or LA would think if they could drink this all the time!" When we declined a second round, Adam's cheery demeanor gave way to a prompt "Here's your check. How do you want to pay?" (He later explained that we were the last table of the night and he was very eager to go home . . .)

A few days later I stopped back in the restaurant with a different friend, Adam still willing to pour us many glasses of delicious, unexpected wine. This time I stayed and chatted with him about an article we had both just read about Shiraz in Iran. I learned more about his vision of elevating the status of Portuguese and Spanish wine, and I was enthralled by his witty and dry humor and his overwhelming passion not only for this great wine, but also for helping the underdogs gain notoriety.

Now, almost two years later, I've joined Adam on his "quests" to visit producers across Portugal and Spain, and I've been fortunate enough to experience his bombastic enthusiasm for really, really good wine that's grown in ways that are good for the environment. I've seen him take chances on wine that most distributors can't or won't buy, I've heard his spiels about the most underrated grapes of the region, and I've learned an unthinkable amount about ideal growing conditions for grape vines.

One of the things I appreciate most about Adam, and what I hope you'll find in this book, is his undying curiosity to learn *why* these wines taste the way they do. What are the ancient techniques being passed down by generations? What are the tools that used to be ubiquitous but are now forgotten? Why don't you see more of this certain type of grape, considering how delicious it is? His thirst for "why" leads him on many adventures, most of which don't go to plan (if there was even a plan to begin with).

The other thing I appreciate about Adam is his unwavering commitment to his own values. He has a unique perspective, an unapologetic but friendly voice, and an unwillingness to humor any pretense. He wants the world to drink better wine, he wants sommeliers to be taken down a notch, he wants producers to plant and harvest grapes in environmentally friendly ways, and he wants the world of wine to be approachable, fun, and simple.

Cheers to embarking on the quest for bomb vinho!

Amy Snook

CEO & FOUNDER, PAREA BOOKS

AUTHOR'S NOTE

Hello and welcome, folks, to this magical quest. My quest, that is, in search of wine. Not just any wine, either, but that good, *good* wine. What I have come to call bomb vinho!

It started as a mere curiosity: I liked the taste. I would hear other people say so too.

"Mmm yeah, this is a gorgeous wine," or, "Fuck me, that's bangin'," from the more struck for words.

But what was it that set one apart from the others? What, I began to wonder, was the formula for perfection?

From there, any attempts to open a door simply led me to another room with more doors. For the last few years, I have been slowly picking through the contents behind each of them, unearthing their secrets, and drinking a fair bit of it too.

My search has since carried me across the globe, then back and forth again numerous times, challenging my definition of home in the process. Which brings us to right here, right now. As I write this, living as I do in one of the beating hearts of the Portuguese wine scene, it all finally seems to be coming together, in a roundabout way.

So let us begin this journey, and in the best place, no less. Not here, in the city of Évora where I now reside, however beautiful it may be. Let's start at The Beginning.

The Beginning

Since I first came to understand the basic story behind wine, I have been hooked. Somehow, this magical liquid can contain so much. It holds within it lessons on culture and tradition as old as time itself. Lessons on geography; the lay of the land. Lessons on chemistry, biology, horticulture, weather, geology, the artistry and history that influenced the planet. All of this, plus a million and one little anecdotes on how things came to be as they are, how they developed a style or flavour or whatever. It's so damn deep!

That captured my attention pretty early on. I already had an interest in all of those separate things, kid with a profound love for my encyclopaedia that I was. And now, all of a sudden, through this one lens I was able to enjoy them all.

This fascination took root at home. My original home, back in New Zealand. As the name may betray, it's pretty fucking new. So too is the way the wine industry operates—because there, that is what it's all about: industry! Given that it is a new country, farmers and investors were not introduced to this novel concept of wine production all that long ago, but when they were, they saw dollar signs. Cut to the bigwigs coming in with all their money and investing in *big* wineries and *big* production.

As a result? The little guy doesn't have much of a look in. There are a few small producers here and there, sure, and they do some great things, but wild innovation and experimentation has not really caught on. Not yet anyway. Still, this provided a great foundation for my interest to grow. The first site being—where else?—the restaurant.

I'll admit I was keen on a bit of pocket money from a tender age, so I got myself a job. "Busting tables" as the big American bossman called it. His name was John and he took me on as an irritating and frequently distracted teen waiter at his busy Mexican restaurant in the small beachside town of Orewa.

"The Sav Blanc is sharp like a lemon and the Chard is big and buttery. Then, this here Pinot is light while the Syrah there has a big body. You got all that?"

Got it.

From there the yarns started spinning. Spinning from a time before I was of legal age to be spinning them and spinning on thereafter, as I finished high school and drifted through university. The restaurants I was working in were getting better—and so was the wine. One joint in particular, known as Orphan's Kitchen in Auckland, shot me forward by a few leagues. We had a cool (and rather global) wine list and, as staff, we were trained on the wines, even tasting the wines together and comparing our findings. Before

I knew it, the wines of different countries were tasting like different things. Oh, that one *did* taste peppery, just like that sales fella said. But which were the good ones? Which were the best ones? And why?

Suddenly, I wasn't so sure.

For the sake of epic storytelling (I am on a quest, remember), let's say it felt to me then as if this was my divine calling. A message from up on high, a bit like with that guy in *The Alchemist*. Then again, now I think it was just some good old-fashioned curiosity, verging on obsession; a need to figure how it all came about, one that's never left me. And it seemed a whole lot better than applying for one of those miserable investment bank positions that the university was trying to waggle enticingly in front of my face.

So, I got a job over the hill behind my parents' place. I grew up in a somewhat rural setting and by this time we were living in a spot that put out a few wines. The name of the region is Matakana, to the north of Auckland, and there are a few nifty little boutique wineries out there, battling against that mental humidity (more on that later). This saw me working the neighbours' vines over the summer with a funny old fella, Richard. He was a good sort, and shared many an insight about vine growing as we traipsed the rows through that hot summer.

Then, as the summer turned to autumn, I found myself with a vintage cellar-hand job at a winery west of Auckland. It was a large estate that produced a wide range of wines from a lot of different varieties and with a load of manual labour. It was hard going. Making wine is not glamorous work, and for me, that vintage was tough (it's possible that I am just a big softy, but it was tough, OK?). It showed me a lot, however. How to treat the different grapes to get the different expressions, as well as many other groovy insights (which I will tell you all about if only you keep reading!).

Mostly, I was on my hands and knees, digging the grapes out of the fermenting tanks, scrubbing them to a high shine, hosing out the massive press:

> "Pump that to the next tank."
> "It better be fucking clean!"

On repeat, 'til the terrifying sounds of rushing water (a good indication that there is a big problem occurring in a winery) were filling my dreams.

Ask anyone who has done some time in the wine industry. It's not easy. I was putting in 12+ hour days, every day, for three months.

Then, finally, the wine was done. As abruptly as it began, it was over.

Not for me though. The very next day I was standing in a foggy field, the property of another winemaking neighbour in the Matakana region, pruning secateurs in hand, learning how to make the winter cuts that would shape the vines' growth the following year.

The thing with wine work, however, is that it's seasonal. As you can probably figure. So what happens when the season is over? When winter has fully closed in and the last cuts of the vineyard's prune have been carefully made?

Well, you switch hemispheres.

This is what led me to begin my adventures abroad: this quest—divine or, more than likely, otherwise—and these adventures are what brought me to Spain and Portugal, where the world and the wine is just a little different. Out here, this is the Old World. For thousands of years people have been cultivating vines and getting rowdy on the delicious wines. And this sentiment is still alive and well. Big business is all around, sure. But in among it there is something special. It seems every person you meet has an aunt, a grandfather, a pet goldfish who owns a plot of land where vines are planted. In a lot of cases, said people have passed on, leaving the vines up for inheritance, or else the owner is just not interested in dealing with them anymore. The fruit is simply going to rot into the ground unless you do something about it. Quite a contrast to the winemaking megafactories of tech-charged NZ.

And this contrast became clear to me right away on arrival. One of the first few trips I took into my new (old) surroundings was to San Sebastián. I was freshly living in Madrid and I had heard very good things. So I jumped on a bus, some high expectations in tow. And I was not disappointed. If you haven't been to the city of San Sebastián, oh man, where to begin . . . The food alone . . . Incredible.

For some reason, that weekend, the pickings for places to stay were slim, which meant I ended up staying in this fuddy-duddy little guest house, a 30-minute walk from the centre. But this landed me closer to the action than expected. The old bloke there, Marco, was well into his garden. He took delight in telling me (all in—at this point for me, unintelligible—Spanish) about all its ins and outs, eventually leading me to his shed, hidden behind some pumpkin vines that were smothering it into oblivion. Here lived his little seedlings that he worked on by the light of a cobweb-strewn window. Something else caught my eye though. I gestured towards it.

"Ahh," he said. "Vino!"

Obscured among some boxes of old magazines were the parts of an old, decaying basket press. One where you turn the handle at the top around and it screws down tighter, pulling out all the juice from the skins. He then pulled out a few more boxes and behind was yet more winemaking paraphernalia. Some old green carboy bottles big enough to hold 50 litres (about 13 gallons), basket-woven up their sides; a box filled with rusty tools and, underneath it all, at the back, a barrel sat, slowly being absorbed by the dust and detritus of the building.

I, for one, thought that was neat. My first trip out and I'd discovered a veteran winemaker? What a find!

Marco wasn't all that fussed though. It turns out Marco's shed isn't unique in the slightest. In fact, it's the same story in every dusty old garage across the land. Here, the means for production are often lying around discarded, free and up for grabs, awaiting rescue. Maybe you just need to replace that little part here or buy that bit there second-hand.

Wherever you go in these parts there will be a relative, a close family friend, or a strange old man who always seems to be sitting on that exact same bench all day, every day, who can come and show you the ropes. And off you go to experiment and innovate. Maybe you make something new, or maybe it's just the way your ancestors did it, following Grandpa's secret family recipe. But there's only going to be a few thousand bottles either way, which someone may well snap up for their hip bar in Amsterdam (as seen in modern days) or often they will sate the village's thirst (a more classic example here)—hardly a picky bunch, but nonetheless enthused. After some more light investigation, I got the feeling that behind every weather-worn little door in every sun-soaked village there is another family secret or local favourite that has been passed through the generations and is still filling their glasses to this day.

OK, maybe I am overembellishing. A little. Of course nothing is ever quite so simple. There's a lot of hard work involved, don't get me wrong (see above labouring). But the opportunity is ripe for the picking—pun intended. And due to this freedom, here in Iberia the world of wine remains fresh, exciting, and adventurous. Things are happening on the forefront, but behind there is even more. The wine culture in these countries goes deep.

There are thousands of grape varieties, or at least differing names in every region, plus a myriad of styles: some leave it in barrel, others in clay; this one is sweet, this guy grows his vines in a wacky way; how about a red wine? This one is white and this one is just a blend of everything that the vineyard had. Sip it, swill it, spill it, laugh, joke, sleep it off, bit of cheese, and then back out to make some more as the weather changes.

I started to really sink my teeth into this world. But what I found was not what I might have expected. What I have mostly found is that . . .

It fuckin' sucks!

Well, on the surface anyway, which is all most of us see. It's just so pretentious. It's a secret club and you didn't get the invite. The gift of a bottle can be a trap to expose how little you know or a simple question may go unanswered forever because one is too embarrassed to ask it.

It's not much of a young gun's game either.

I can still remember one of the first wine tasting events that I was invited to by one of the local distributors in NZ. I was around 18 and fresh faced. As we gathered in the lobby of their office, I noticed that I was the only youngster among a group of 50- to 60-year-old men. And they were keen to show my inexperience. One proceeded to make a joke about the coffee I had in my hand and how I had already ruined the tasting for myself, much to the other guys' mirth. That's how a lot of it has been. Standing among groups of circle-jerking older men who all seek to outdo each other with their superior knowledge, all the while revealing just how much money they have to blow on great wine (or so the label says, right?).

And this brings me to what I have always found most peculiar. Within the wine world there's this bizarre transformation that occurs. The people presenting the wine are too often these stuck up, elitist knobheads who, instead of helping you to make your selection, just seek to alienate you with the amount they know, all without ever letting you in on "the big secret."

Where does this transformation come from?

Why is the dinner table so far from the vineyards, so to speak?

And who inserts the silver spoon up into place? Seemingly, it's BYO.

I find sommelierism to be the same. I have worked in restaurants, most recently at an awesome place called Restaurant SEM in Lisbon (eat there, it's good!). There I preferred to call myself the wine manager, as a sommelier and all that implies is not really what I want to be. I don't give a fuck what glass you think this wine should be served in. Oh, and you were able to recognise an Albariño in a blind-tasting? Ooh cool, fuck off!

Side note. What is the fascination with blind tasting anyway? Cool party trick I guess, but it's only useful on the off chance we uncover a Caribbean haul of sunken wine which holds the secrets of the earth that can save us from a near inevitable destruction. Oh no, the label has washed away, whatever will we do? Bring in the blind tasters! They'll save us!

Until then, I'm fine just reading the label, thanks.

The same goes for glasses. I enjoy a nice wine glass but I also believe a good wine will taste good in a mug. Appreciate all your attempts to intellectually intimidate me, though. Fun times.

Like the time I was being shown how to serve wine the "proper way" by another waiter who had "worked at a Michelin star gaff." The genius proceeded to cut the foil in a jagged fashion that sliced his finger open. As his blood started to seep, I tried using the good old, improper method instead. The customers were happy, slurping away. My fingers remained intact.

That's not what we are here for though. This isn't where wine comes from. While making the wine, there's not a bow tie in sight. These people—these winemakers—are farmers! Wrapped in overalls stained a new colour every harvest, they spend their days toiling in the vineyards and wineries, hands filthy and cracked, the sweat glistening on their brows as they pursue their craft. They are creatives, yes, but not in the romanticised way we think. From personal experience, I can say it's hard fucking graft and once one has had a go, they never see a glass of wine the same way. It takes a certain type of madness to be a winemaker. Because it takes a little madness and a lot of willingness to wait the long time that's needed to discover the fruits of all this labour.

So, let's have a go.

These are my adventures across the Iberian Peninsula, as well as a few factoids thrown in here and there, on my quest for bomb vinho! With this book, I show where the wine is actually from, as well who makes it, and share the stories I have come across.

Am I a master winemaker? No. How many wine qualifications do I have? Zero.

But what I do have is experience. Experience I have picked up from all of the places I have seen (and sipped): in wineries, vineyards, restaurants, shops, and offices all over the world. I've been a cellar-hand, vineyard hand, exporter, marketer, restaurant wine manager, forklift licence holder, consultant, tractor driver, guy with the shovel, and general fanatic.

This is what I have discovered along the way.

CONTENTS

PART TWO

IN YOUR GLASS

FOREWORD

It was December 2021 in not-so-wintery Lisbon, barely six months after SEM opened its doors. The restaurant was winding down from an incredibly busy first summer when we found ourselves without a sommelier. As you do in a city like Lisbon, where the degree of separation tends to stay below two, we met Adam through friends. "We have a friend who works with wine, and he's also a Kiwi!" To most people, the latter is a seemingly uninteresting addendum, but with there being only fifty New Zealanders living in the whole of Portugal at the time, our interest was piqued and we hit it off, straight off the bat.

But at the time, Adam was happily employed at a wine bar and had no need for another job. Still, in those first weeks of meeting we hung out, we talked wine, we chatted stories about the homeland, traded tales about living abroad, and we drank. A lot. There are memories of nights at Tati Wine Bar with bills that mirrored the wine list, cheap beers at the local tasca and faint recollections of Lara's birthday party, that may or may not have ended in an out-of-hand lock-in at SEM . . .

And then the message came. "Hey, is that job offer still going or has the ship sailed?" The ship was very much still anchored—the job was his and we were stoked.

Ours is not an obvious restaurant. We eschew convention and we don't compromise on our reason for being. Bound by our determination to see value where others don't, our cuisine is the coming together of creative thinking, a vow never to discard, and a commitment to nature. Our operational model is constructed so as to evaluate the environmental impact of every decision we make. A little bit ruthless, a little bold, definitely experimental. And our wine programme had to do just that. Adam's job description was simple, yet, nevertheless challenging when you operate in the scope that is the natural wine world in a small country: make our wine list personal to SEM.

We didn't want a sommelier. We wanted someone whose passion for wine could be visible on their skin. We wanted someone with the right mix of knowledge and bravado, who knew where to find the producers doing interesting, out-of-the-ordinary wines not yet on anyone else's list. We wanted someone who did not conform, because we have never. We wanted someone with charisma and initiative, who excelled at delivering a wine pairing or suggesting a banger of a glass, and not with grandeur or ostentation, but with ingenuity, eloquence, and good banter. The answer was Adam.

He delivered on his job description, and then some. His ferociously unique look at wine, matched with utmost respect of the winemakers, his big frame, booming voice, and his very personal style, is one hell of a combo. It ruffles the feathers of the old school and feels relatable and refreshing to the new. We're proud and happy that SEM in turn could simultaneously be a platform for his narrative and a chapter on his adventure.

Bravo, Adam.

And here's to the glass of whatever we drink together next.

Lara & George

SEM RESTAURANT / LISBON, PORTUGAL

THE JOURNEY: A BIRD'S-EYE VIEW

So, you're still with me then?

Good.

Full disclosure. There's not exactly going to be a straight up chronology to the coming journey, or journeys, I should say. These are the many wonderful things about wine I have come across, yes, but all from a large number of small forays, spanning a number of years. I'll give you a brief outline now though, so you get the gist of where I've been (and where we'll be going). Perhaps we can draw a little map to accompany us!

When I first came over from NZ in 2016, I went to work a vintage (the term used for the winemaking period) for a young guy called Alex in the tiny, French town of Peyriac-de-Mer in the southern region of Languedoc. It was my first time producing bonafide handmade wine and it gave me a taste for it.

Then I decided Spain was more my flavour. I moved to set up camp in Madrid, where I worked for a number of producers over the years in places like Jumilla, Méntrida, Almansa, and eventually the Terra Alta. Many trips were made to these and surrounding areas.

I made the move out to the Terra Alta region in 2019, to the town of Batea, although soon after, the Covid bomb dropped and the world changed. I got a few good trips in here, before the global shutdown. But soon, the reality of being in a very tiny, isolated town in Catalunya hit me. I needed a move.

Many a summer had already been spent over the border and I was eager to uncover the mysteries waiting there. In short, Portugal was calling. A few days after Christmas of 2020, I landed in Lisbon, once again with my whole life on my back.

Since living in Portugal, I have really dug in deep. My thirst is never sated! My time spent with the amazing folks at Restaurant SEM shot me forward by leap years in valuable experience. And now I am lucky enough to have found a partner, Amy, who shares in my desire for endless adventures (and good wine).

We toured the Priorat, Montsant, and Terra Alta one autumn. Mid-winter, we headed through shrouds of fog and heavy rain to La Rioja, Ribera del Duero, and Rueda. There was also a quick trip to Cádiz and Jerez de la Frontera, and then a spring visit to the Canary Islands where we saw the wild shit going down on Tenerife and Lanzarote. Summer tripping, we have found ourselves exploring the Beira, Bairrada, and Dão regions. Are you following?

After some time in Lisbon and seeking a change of scenery, Amy and I made a more permanent move to the city of Évora, capital of the Alentejo region. From here we do a lot of touring, always on the trail for more. Most recently, we headed up to the Douro Valley and got better acquainted with the Vinho Verde region. Trippin' and sippin', as the old saying goes. Well, mine.

Beyond the actual trips though, I have spent many hours over all these years pouring over books and websites on all subjects related to wine and its producers and pouring plenty of bottles in the process: another important means of fact-checking. This information has helped me make sense of all my own experiences, connect the dots, and paint the bigger picture for you here, as best I can.

It is thanks to all these adventures, the physical and the literary, as well as many more (I'm sure there are some I have forgotten—that can happen with wine) that I may finally, *finally* begin.

PART ONE

OF THE EARTH

Good wine is the product of good land. But not just any land. There is a special recipe for success when it comes to selecting the best patch to plant your vines and all factors, of which there are many, are considered.

But what are they exactly? You may ask.

Well indulge me for a while.

Are you sitting quite comfortably?

Alright, so first and foremost . . .

You may recall from "The Journey" my brief mention of a little place called Jumilla. Not Spain's most famous region by a long shot, but definitely one that deserves our attention.

It is a small but significant winemaking region sitting in the eastern-central part of Spain, just inland of Alicante. While living in Madrid, I spent some time working remotely for a producer out there. He wasn't too interested in showing me much of where the wine comes from, but he was interested in me selling it (go figure).

Still, I was keen to learn more as I had, for one, tasted good things in their favourite grape variety, as well as other, not-so-good things made of this same variety from other places nearby. What made the difference?

The variety I am referring to? Monastrell. This smooth cat goes by a few other names, such as Mourvedre in France or Mataro in Australia (odd considering the town of Mataro is near Barcelona), and is a big deal in the region of Jumilla and those that surround it. The folks here reckon it's the cat's pyjamas, so it makes up over 80 percent of the region's production. These guys are going all in.

The wine is wicked though, so it does make some sense. The ones from Jumilla, anyway. They are full bodied, dark inky purple, super fuckin' velvety and they tingle with these really soft chalky tannins.

Now, I've tasted a few Monastrells from other parts and they range from sort-of-OK to just-plain-meh. And even when it is good . . . it's just not the same, you know? So, what's the deal here? Why are those specific to Jumilla so damn good? (Mandatory shout out to Yecla and Bullas—I know you're keeping it real with the Monastrell too.) There was only one thing to do. I had to jump on a train to Alicante.

Impulse soon saw me speeding east from Madrid, where I was struck by the barren plains of central Spain. The soil of this part of the country is rich in iron clay, meaning it burns with an intense terracotta red only punctuated by the light greens of the little vineyards, grown close to the ground, and the darker greens of the holm oaks that dot the landscape. The land started to change, however, as we zoomed downhill to Alicante. The view from the train window became almost entirely engulfed in green under a bright blue sky. Beautiful stuff, but not the destination. From Alicante, I more or less had to retrace my steps, heading out of the city and inland again on a bus, thinking all the while that this place had better be worth it. Once boarded, we were almost immediately climbing back upwards.

See, Jumilla sits on the side of a cliff, climbing all the way up to the central plateau of Spain. This particular cliff forms a rim around the edge of the country where it meets the Mediterranean, from near Tarragona all the way to Murcia. I have heard it referred to by the locals as *el Balcón del Mediterráneo*, "the balcony to the Mediterranean," due to the way that it towers, like a shelf, over the sea. Its highest points are over 1000 metres (over 3300 feet) above sea level. Jumilla is located on this slope, leading up the balcony.

And as the bus weaved between the small villages lining the road to our destination, we gradually got higher. After an hour or so, when I finally stepped off the bus into downtown Jumilla, we were already at an altitude of 500 metres (about 1600 feet). Jumilla is a pretty little town. Like the scores around it, it's all dusty sandstone buildings with terracotta tiled roofs that get denser and denser as you approach the central church. Up on the overlooking hill, the castle sits removed, keeping an eye over the tightly packed buildings below.

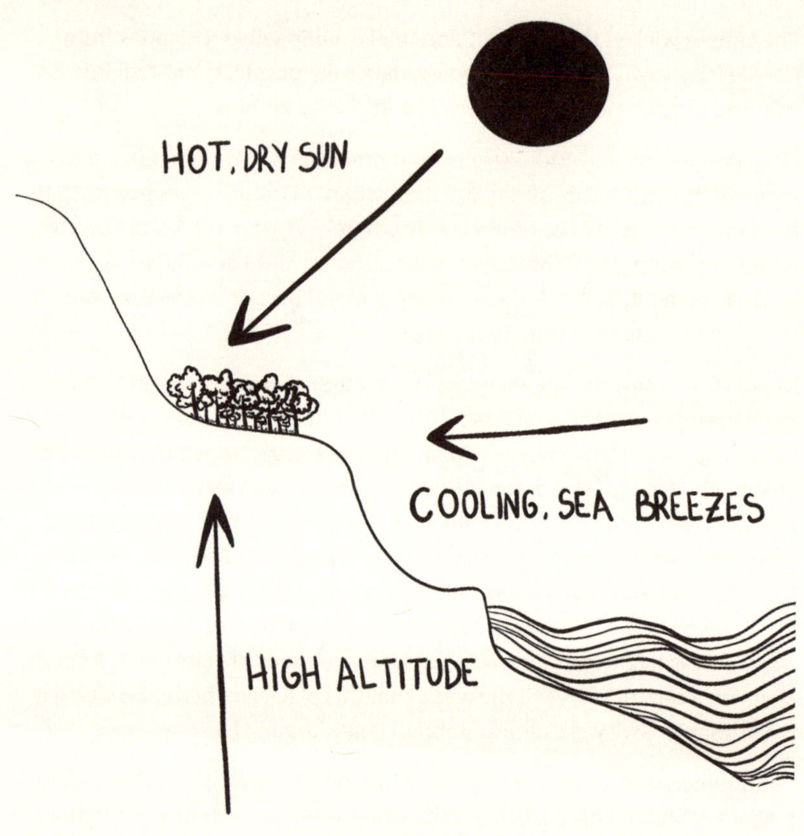

I didn't have much of a plan from the bus stop. My only plan, in fact, was to crash in one of the little hostels round the corner, so that was sorted. What next though? Scanning the map on my phone, I noticed a cluster of wineries not far out of town. I grabbed some water (essential in these parts) and started to pound the pavement, fed up with all other forms of transport for one day. It was good and hot. Not even late spring but the dial said 26 degrees (nearly 79 degrees F), neither a cloud in sight nor a breeze of any kind. The air was bone dry too. I spent the afternoon walking among some of the vineyards. I even stopped in at one of the wineries for a little solo tasting and grabbed a bottle of my favourite for later—a delicious Monastrell, in case you didn't guess. It was a pleasant afternoon. Ooh and I saw a fox. Thumbs up, Jumilla. Still, this wasn't exactly what I'd come for.

But nothing else of note was happening. A long way to come for a bottle of wine, even for me. Pleasantly tipsy, yet presently none the wiser, I started to worry that this had been a fool's errand. That was until after dinner.

I had later picked at some tapas standing in one of the bars, sipped a few *cañas* (little beers), and shaken my head at some football that was catching fellow patrons' attention on the screen. Be sure to do this if you ever find yourself in Spain. Essential tourism tip, right there. Anyway, walking back to my little hostel I noticed it was pretty darn chilly. The air had cooled down. Right down. Now, the temperature gauge was saying 15 degrees (59 degrees F) and there was going to be a low that night of 11 (52 F)!

OK, so not that dramatic, I'll admit. But in that moment I had a realisation. The Monastrells that weren't doing it for me were often from lower-lying Alicante, while the ones that were came from up here in Jumilla, where the vineyards range from 400 to 800 metres (1300 to 2600 feet) above sea level. The climate is continental, so it gets pretty hot and dry, with the area experiencing a decent amount of drought (although the chalky, clay soils help a lot with moisture retention) AND, to top it all off, it's right next to the coast. The breezes that come in from the sea, often blowing through the evening and night, keep the temperatures low when the sun isn't up.

This combination is not too rare in winemaking regions, but Jumilla's is particularly punchy—and it really helps that Monastrell along. The grapes in this eastern area of the country make for a great case study on the influence of varying climates. A tasty case study.

Because my trip to Jumilla told me that this indeed was the secret. The holy trifecta! DIURNAL MOTHERFUCKIN' SHIFT at its best.

What the hell is that, you ask? OK, let's get into it . . .

I want to start this book off with a bang by talking about the baddest meteorological phenomenon in all the land! It's not the hottest or the chillest but the difference between the two that gives this badass its power. I mean what's not to love right? Are you not just freaking out right now? I am.

Wait. Maybe I should tell you what it is first.

By definition, diurnal shift is the average change between the daytime temperatures and the temperatures at night, and it's this phenomenon that is responsible for the best quality wine grapes. To make good wine, you have to have good fruit. No way around it.

They say that the best wine is made in the vineyard and it's true. The characteristics of good grapes are ripe, mature, fruity flavours balanced with the right amount of acidity. And this word, balance, is the key to quality wines. It needs to be struck between the fruit, the tannin, the alcohol, but most importantly the acidity: this is what cuts through the mouth, keeping the wine tidy, poised and fresh on the tongue, not allowing any of the big flavours to dawdle or become stale on the palate.

And how do you get this balance in your grapes? Well, by not cooking the living fuck out of them on the vines. That's how.

This is where our good, good friend DIURNAL SHIFT comes in.

So again, this difference between day and night temperatures is crucial. And we want it to be as high as possible, meaning a healthy amount of heat during the day, which then dips down to some chilly chills in the night. This process brings about a slow cook effect for the grapes. Each day, over the course of the ripening season, the grapes will heat up in the sun, promoting their ripening, and at night it's as if they're being put on ice when temperatures plummet again, slowing everything down. Then the next day the sun has to work a lot harder to warm them up again and continue their ripening.

As a result, grapes mature over a much longer period of time, building in complexity and depth of flavour, while also helping retain their acidity as they ripen. Under these conditions, grapes tend to be a lot deeper in colour, have a lot more tannin and a more developed fruit character than those produced in areas without the shift.

When produced in climates that stay warm all through the night, grapes mature rapidly, causing all that acidity to get burned up in the process. Like cooking a cake on too high a temperature, it burns on the outside and stays mush in the middle. The grapes are the same: getting overcooked outside while, inside the grape, the ripening lags behind. The resulting fruit will often be lacking quality, depth, and complexity. AKA *no bueno*. Not what we're looking for.

So this is why we like DIURNAL SHIFT. It helps us and our taste buds out a lot. But where do we find it?

The ideal sites for this phenomenon are either up high or where it is really dry, for example up on the mountainside, or in any area where there is a bit of altitude, where the wind whistles and things get chilly when the sun dips. Also in drier areas, where there is little or no humidity for temperatures to cling to. As they say, it's cold in the desert. Coasts too, bring about a fair bit of this, especially the wild Atlantic edges of Portugal and Spain.

This is why grapes, at least the best ones, are always grown in high, dry, or coastal places.

It's all down to motherfuckin' DIURNAL SHIFT!!

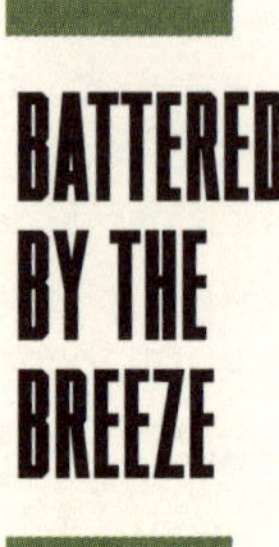

What a special place, old Bairrada. This little region is somewhat overlooked at times, flanked by the Douro and Dão regions, with Lisbon sitting below. It may be small but it's doing its thing and what it is doing is remarkable—and pretty unique for Portugal.

As with the entire western coast of Portugal, Bairrada is battered by the wild and harsh Atlantic Ocean. The ocean is icy cold even on a summer's day and brings brazen winds that whip the land and lash it with licks of salt. A huge effect is had on the soil here and, as a result, the wines. It sits there almost like a little saucer, ready to receive whatever the ocean dishes up. The surrounding land gently rolls with little rises and valleys, all ringed by high hills to the east, at the top of which sits the Dão plateau. These overlooking hills form a microclimate, blocking any heat drifting from further inland and keeping the region cool. As a result, the area below is humid and salty with lots of rain and thick blankets of fog that roll in and out as they wish. One afternoon driving down that coast, my friends and I watched as within a few minutes the air had bundled itself together in a dense cloud and rolled across the road in front of us, obscuring our vision beyond a few metres.

We had cobbled together an impromptu road trip. I had been in the city of Porto at a wine event and they were driving past in a van, heading south towards Lisbon, where I was living at the time. I suggested the Bairrada region as a good place to check out along the way. So, we camped for a night among some vines. However, the only clothes I had were the ones I was wearing: jeans, boots, and a thick button-down. I was lucky to have a jumper with me too, and I felt said luck keenly when that night the temperatures dropped. I remember seeing my breath by torchlight as I set up our tent with ice-cold fingers.

But by morning, the sun comes out and warms the place up. That I can tell you for sure. It was barely 10 a.m. when I was somewhat regretting my heavy clothes. It only got hotter as we proceeded to visit a winery or two, sweat marking our backs. At the afternoon's end we were back on the road south, by which time all the sun's hard work was already being blown away by onshore winds, just as it started to dip behind the horizon.

Needless to say, this little place is ripe with—say it with me—DIURNAL SHIFT.

Yet that is not the only trick in Bairrada's arsenal. It has some pretty neat geology underlying it too.

At some point the sea would have washed across this whole area. This means that below the surface the dirt is rich with great veins of limestone that can reach 10 kilometres (33 feet) inland. Limestone, mixed in with the clay, holds a lot of water within it, yet allows any excess to wash away, leaving the vines with comfortable amounts of hydration year-round. It's also associated with producing wines of biting acidity and sharp minerality. These conditions put up some harsh resistance for ripening grapes, so some special locals have had to learn how to adapt.

Struggling under such humid conditions, the old vines of this region are fascinating. Over a hundred years old, they grow with long spindly arms to a height of around 1.5 metres (5 feet). The new vines are grown in similar fashion, in tall upright rows to safeguard against too much moisture. In fact, it's these unique and rather difficult conditions that have lent a hand in developing some cool grape varieties.

The main offender goes by the name of Baga. These grapes have weathered it all and come out on top. Thin-skinned and zinging with acidity, when made into red wine these little fellas develop balsamic fruit and a leathery minerality with the most elegant of structures. Similar to Pinot Noir or Nebbiolo, they are truly exceptional.

But the more famous output of the region would probably have to be the sparkling. Because of these conditions (a big DIURNAL SHIFT, sea salt, and the bolt of limestone), the grapes have difficulty achieving ripeness. They are green and full of acid, meaning they've grown under perfect conditions for making great sparkling wine. Baga does a lot to help out too! Shout out to the other regional champs: the white grapes Bical and Cercial, which have also been honed by these same conditions to produce lightning acidity and crunchy minerality. Nice one, guys.

Bairrada is a region with so many wicked wines though, all combining to change the commonly lacklustre narrative around Portuguese winemaking. Not only that, but it is a true champion of the DIURNAL SHIFT!

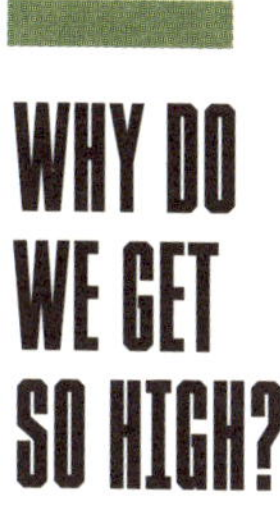

WHY DO WE GET SO HIGH?

Everywhere you look in the wine industry there is always something to be bragged about. One that comes up a fair bit when people talk about the "privileged" terroir they use to grow their grapes is the altitude. The vines are grown up high, on the hillside or mountainside, and this always comes into their marketing, or at the very least the story of why *their* wines are better.

Is it just for the stunning views that one gets from these picturesque vineyards? While I am a real sucker for big sweeping vistas from up a mountain range, there may be a little more to it than that.

The high altitude provides a lot of unique benefits to grape production that can enhance the quality of the wine and at the very least can give it some unique characteristics. The first of these is to do with that chilly mountain breeze that sets in as the sun dips. We all know what that means, right?

Cool temps at night, and hot ones in the day! Ca-ching, it's DIURNAL SHIFT!

In the mountains, it's not just any old hot either, which brings me to the next benefit: mountain heat is a special heat. Up higher, where the atmosphere is thinner, there are more UV rays. On ground level, there is more atmosphere, which blocks a lot of them. At altitude, however, less blockage means more can pass through, hitting the grapes. These grapes with higher UV exposure toughen up by developing thicker skins. This brings about a deeper colour concentration and a more pronounced tannin.

There's also the benefit of extra drainage. Grapes require some water to survive but we don't want them drinking in too much (I'll explain why a bit later). With a bit of altitude and incline there is more gravity to pull the water away, meaning less for the vine. Less water also brings about a higher flavour concentration, as there is reduced dilution, so these wines can often have a richer and more robust profile.

Another benefit here would be higher ventilation. In these high places the wind tends to whip, which keeps the grapes dry. Humidity is the real enemy with grapes. Too much of it brings about a whole host of diseases that will ruin the crop, so a stiff breeze will keep them dry and healthy.

In summary, on the mountainside there is a lot less water retention, the water flowing down with gravity, so the roots are drier, the skins are thicker, the grapes are healthier, and the wine is stronger. Boom!

Grow your grapes on a hill, folks.

Or, you know, don't. Whatever you like.

LA MESETA AND HOW IT SAVES THE DAY!

In the chapter about the ever-legendary DIURNAL SHIFT, we talked a bit about how dry weather works in favour of a high swing in temperatures. This is because moisture, when suspended in the air, tends to have a warming effect, thanks to its ability to hold onto heat. Basically, the more humid areas are not cooling down a whole lot at night. Super dry places are better for this—but then they aren't exactly ideal either. I mean, how much wine do you see growing in the desert?

For a good DIURNAL SHIFT, we want the air to be drier than it is humid, but we still need a bit of that precious water to sate the vines' thirst. Also, and probably more importantly, the higher the temperatures get when things are really hot and dry, the more the ground will continue to radiate lots of heat throughout the night. Temperatures will take a dive, as deserts are known to, but the ground temperature is going to keep the vines warm long into the night. Plus, the intensity of that heat is going to produce fast-ripening grapes, regardless of a nocturnal dip in temperatures.

This would be the case for Spain too if it weren't for a particular detail that saves the damn day! Well, better than just the day—it's what makes it a place that's actually capable of producing the epic fucking wine it does. The Iberian Peninsula is a hot one and the arid centre of Spain is where the heat just bakes and bakes. Miles from any coastal influences, regions like Castilla-La Mancha, the world's largest wine region, have little chance of any nocturnal cooling which would turn this place into a real-life desert.

But thankfully, we can raise a toast instead to La Meseta—the massive high-altitude plateau that makes up central Spain. See Spain, covered in flat plains as it is, is actually for the most part at high altitudes. The average is 650 metres (2100 feet) above sea level, with the capital city of Madrid sitting more or less right on that mark. In fact, the whole Iberian Peninsula is characterised by this sprawling shelf of land situated up above, like a tabletop, meaning the coastal regions often sit at the base of giant cliffs.

You'll remember this from our earlier trip to Jumilla, which sits on the rise up to this shelf, stretching across the entire centre of Spain. Beyond Jumilla, heading west, the climb continues until it peaks and you find yourself looking across the plains of another wine region where I have spent some time, called Almansa. The interesting thing about Almansa is that it marks the edge of the shelf. At an altitude of 700 metres (2300 feet), the conditions here are dramatically different to those below.

Again, I touched on this when talking about Jumilla: on the cliffside heading down to the sea there is more water. Not a lot more—Jumilla still experiences plenty of drought—but enough to see a difference. It is greener. And it continues becoming more so as you near the coast. Almansa, on the edge of the shelf, however, is where the land turns to red and orange, like a scene from the Wild West. This central plateau is steep sided, with high cliffs, all the way around the eastern coast. To the south, the region of Andalucia acts like a large ramp, starting at sea level along the southern coast and rising to 500 metres (1600 feet) above on its northern border, where it meets Castilla-La Mancha. In the north of Spain, the huge mountain range known as the Cordillera Cantábrica rises out of the sea to the plateau. Then, to the west, Portugal too gradually increases in altitude to where it borders with Spain.

Where am I going with all this? Well, if you haven't guessed it, all roads here lead to one place. This awesome geographic fact dictates the climates

A Topographical Cross Section of Iberia

(more or less)

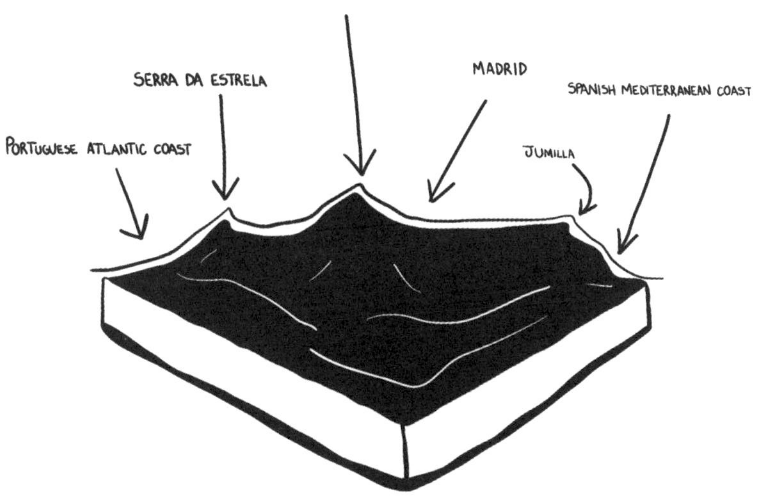

responsible for—what else?—the incredible wines produced across La Meseta. The hot centre of Spain would be more like the Sahara, which doesn't sit all too far away, if it weren't for the plateau's heights. During the day temperatures soar but at night they plummet as powerful winds sweep through, rushing down from the even higher mountains or across from the river valleys, gifting the whole peninsula with so many places for unique and notably excellent wine production.

The mountain ranges and cliffs encircling the centre likewise provide prime geographic conditions for wine production along the steep coasts, while in the middle, various mountain systems and rivers create unique pockets of land that roast in the day, freeze at night, and succumb to significant temperature shifts between the seasons. All in all, this makes for a perfect wine growing country, which is indeed how Spain has earned its reputation as a producer of amazing, robust reds that course with powerful acidity.

And all thanks to the high altitude of that central plateau. A hero to us all.

There are many peaks and summits across the great Meseta. But to me, there is one place that felt really special. In the very centre of Spain, to the west of the capital, lies the Sistema Central, a huge rift of mountains that, rising high, slash the country in two. Within these towering ranges is the Sierra de Gredos. It's just a little region, dwarfed by the massive band of mountains surrounding it—but it is an exceptional little region.

Like many parts of Spain, it used to be prolific in the viticulture scene. Vineyards would line the mountainsides and the towns (and townspeople) would be stained red with a seemingly never-ending flow of wine. Economic decline saw all that melt away in the 20th century. Most of the vineyards were uprooted to be replanted with pine trees, whose wood fetched a good price without much maintenance. Thankfully, a number of winemakers are still hanging on in the Sierra de Gredos. In truth what I discovered, up there on the top of the world, is that they're still thriving. What remains of the vineyards are stunning old, twisted vines of Garnacha and Albillo Real, among others, that produce elegant, focused wines with keen acidity.

Amy and I had a wonderful trip through the region where we came across some breath-taking spots. Jesús Soto Esteban, who goes by the name Chuchi, was one of our very generous guides. Based in the town of Cebreros, he makes some spectacular wines, under the name SotoManrique, from his small plots dotted around the hills and peaks soaring above the small town. He took us out to see a few one autumn afternoon.

As we left Cebreros, the climb started immediately, with us zigzagging our way up the steep bank, until we eventually veered off the road and headed down a dusty little track. Here we were met with a stone wall. Beyond this wall were the vines occupying one of his many plots, not even his highest, that sloped off down the hill. This vineyard, he told us, is called Laderas de la Mira, "hillside of the sight" or "lookout," as a rough translation. Walking through the vines, the soils loose with slate and quartz glistening in the setting sunlight, it was easy to see why it was named after its view.

The bank started gradually by the roadside but then sloped down steeply towards the lower edge of the vineyard. And from that edge, almost directly below, as if we could bungee jump our way back down there, was the town of Cebreros. We were on the top shelf, it seemed. The vineyard sitting at over 1000 metres (3300 feet) above sea level; the town at 750 (2500). The wine Chuchi produces from the patch is pretty top shelf too, the slate and quartz lending it a dark concentration of colour and balsamic depth that dances with bright acidity.

Chuchi's wasn't the only remarkable vineyard we came across on our trip either. We were staying in the town of El Barraco, which sits not far to the west of Cebreros. The host of our accommodation, after a bit of wine chit-chat, mentioned that there were a couple of young folks in town doing some cool stuff and that we should try to link up. It turned out they were names we were already familiar with, Nahuel Ibarra and Vicky Sanchez, who run the project Pequeños y Salvajes out there in the mountains known as the Gredos, and who also make some ace wines.

Similar to Chuchi, they work with small patches of old vines and they have a growing list of people who are eager to give them their fruit. We visited one of their special vineyards, this stunning little valley, full of all kinds of fruit trees but also loads of beautiful, gnarled old vineyards that Nahuel says were well over 150 years old.

"We have a lot of opportunities to work the abandoned vineyards of this region, which allows us to be picky," he told us, an excited glow in his eyes above a huge beam stretching from ear to ear. "We only work with the really special ones. Where we are here is over 1000 [3300 feet] of altitude: we don't bother with anything below that mark. We love the precision and focus that the altitude gives the wine from these old vines. So much complexity!"

The stories of Chuchi, Nahuel, and Vicky taught me some remarkable things about the wine production taking place amidst the world's summits, while the wines themselves were sensational. There's definitely some method to their high-altitude madness.

It doesn't always have to be so high, though. Sometimes the valley is where it's at.

Altitude is a big deal. It has a large effect on what we can produce. Clearly, coasts are good too. There's another feature though that is highly common to the world's great wine regions. And that is the river.

Rivers are a bold and beautiful feature of the land. For millennia before, they have twisted and turned through the landscape. What started as a trickle has built and built, cutting through solid stone and washing away the dust to carve a determined path to the sea. To civilization, they bring essential resources in the forms of water and food. They are also handy for transport and trade.

And then they are often lined with these famous wine regions. Have a think now as to how many of these regions are dominated by a mighty river that cuts it in two. I can surely think of a handful. The Rhone, Loire, and Sâone in France; the Mösel in Germany; and of course, the Douro/Duero, the Ebro, and the Tejo in Iberia. These and many more.

So, what *do* rivers bring to winemaking? A number of things actually.

First, a little story. Once, on a trip with some friends from Madrid, we found ourselves in the beautiful city of Sevilla. One of the gems of the south, this city teems with history, and signs of the country's former, very extreme wealth are evident. It was July, however, so exploration was a challenge. This is because the city is like a furnace. For most of summer, daytime temperatures soaring well into the 30s and 40s (high 80s to low 100s F) are very common. Because of this, one must generally lay low during the summer days, awaiting the evening.

On this occasion we were staying in the centre of town near to the big mushroom-like wooden canopy, quite aptly named Las Setas de Sevilla (*seta* = mushroom). When the dark was finally upon us, we ventured out. The heat was still thick in the air as we walked the central streets, where we heard there was a fiesta on the other side of town, so we made a beeline.

The fiesta turned out to be the annual Fiesta del Barrio Triana (the Triana neighbourhood party, no less). Triana sits on the western side of the city and it pushes up against the Guadalquivir, the famous river of Spanish antiquity that links the city to the Mediterranean Sea. The street along the river's edge was packed with people and lined with tents that were striped with green and white. It was still pretty hot and the cold glasses of beer and gazpacho awaiting us there were very welcome.

As the night wore on though, this started to change. A wind had arisen, coming down the river from the north; it was just a gentle breeze but all of a sudden there was this cool sting to the air. Enough to stop the sweat forming on everyone's brow as the party continued. After an hour or two, we decided to head back towards our accommodation in search of a late (for us, not for the Spanish) dinner. But back among the buildings, away from the river, the heat picked up again and we were soon back to sweating as we walked the streets in the still summer night.

So, what is it that makes rivers useful for the viticulturists?

One, that I hope should be bloody obvious by now, is the ever-so-legendary DIURNAL SHIFT. In the hot regions of central Portugal and Spain, as you can probably expect, a large body of water moving swiftly through the valley is going to bring a temperature-lowering effect. As the night comes, the changing temperatures can alter the pressure systems of the area, bringing winds that will slice through the river's valley. These winds pick up any moisture that has evaporated into the air, supplying the desired

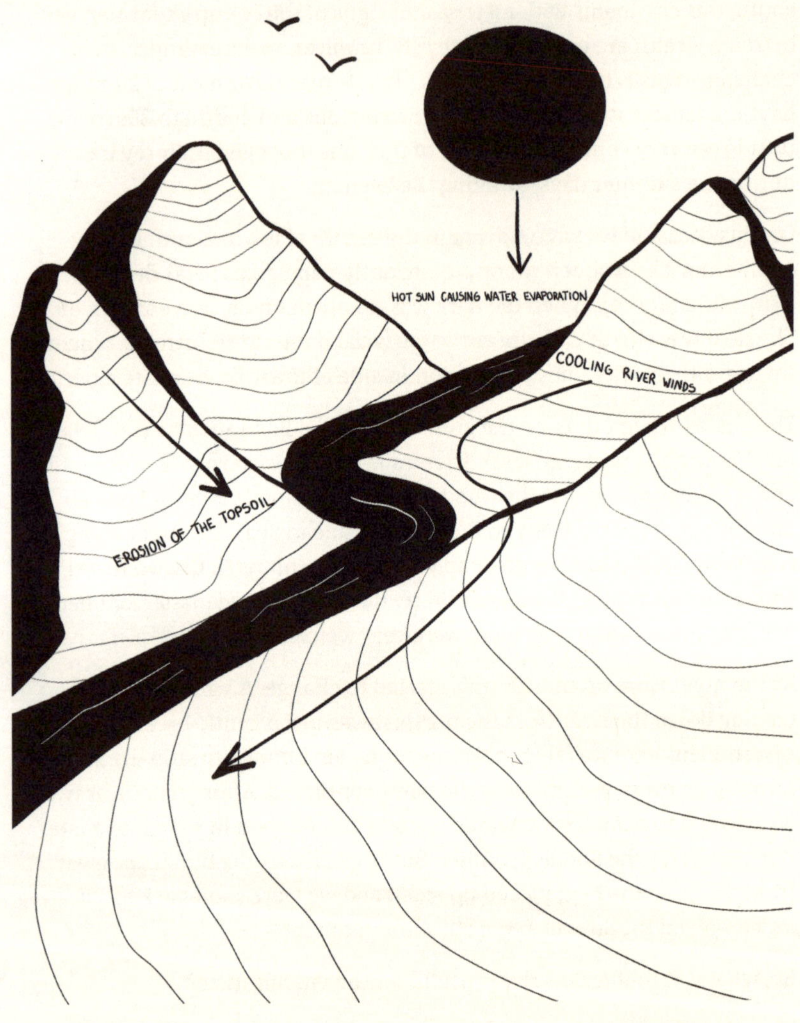

cooling effect as the collected water works to chill that wind down. The steep, terraced valleys, often where the vines are planted, also act as holding tanks for all this humidity, which, once the night falls, turns to dew. Like the sweat on your brow on a hot summer night, this cools down the air around the vines.

As we know from our now extensive DIURNAL SHIFT expertise, the cool nights help to lock in acidity and build complexity within grapes. In hot climates, the presence of the river is often the defining factor that shapes the wine up, taking it from flabby, stewed plonk to a crisp, structured beauty. The rivers also do a lot for cold climes too, making a pretty good go of keeping things warm—or at least warmer.

Imagine the valley again. Without the river, there is no other force to counteract the cold: it will bite down deep in the ground and there it will stay. With the river, however, there is a moving body of water that holds its temperature, which is much above freezing thanks to its high heat capacity, that is, the capacity for a substance to absorb heat without experiencing a change in temperature. For example, iron changes temperature at a rate eight times greater than water does. This means the water moving through the valley has heat trapped therein, stopping it from freezing and acting as a sort of heater to the valley around it.

Additionally, the river is said to act as a sun mirror for the vines. As the sun shines during the day, the light cast on the surface of the water is reflected onto the surrounding slopes, adding just a little more warmth during the day.

So, the river is good at cooling hot and heating cool but it's also just good for general balance. It has been noted that regions divided by a river experience less fluctuations in temperature. As if the river takes the edge off, absorbing what is not needed to level things out. Go river!

And then there is the geology. Rivers like to pick things up, carry them along, and drop them somewhere else. They've probably done this with your straw hat that got blown off when you were out for a leisurely punt, but they also do this to the soil. At the bottom of the valley, they cut up the bedrock and cart the dust off to sea. As the valley gets deeper, silt and organic matter is also dragged away wherever the river's water touches.

Then there is the rain. Around the rivers, due to the heating and cooling of masses of water that occurs here, there is a fair amount of precipitation. Over millions of years this rain flows down the banks, each time shifting off more and more of the loose silt and organic matter and leaving behind just the hard heavy stone. The banks and surrounding areas that slope down to the rivers are, as a result, stripped of all fertile soil, leaving just

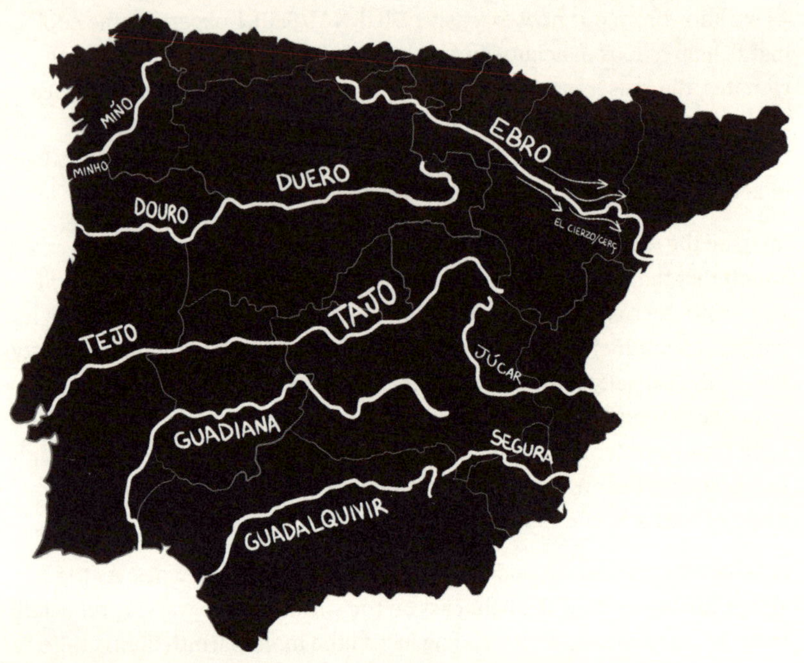

the bare bones, the tough, gritty stone. There's no vegetable that will grow here; there are no nutrients for that. Ahh but what about the wine?

Let's dip into some of the more individual characteristics of some of the major rivers of Iberia, namely, the Duero (in Spanish) or Douro (in Portuguese), the Ebro, and the Tejo (in Portuguese, Tagus in Spanish).

WHEN THE DUERO BECOMES THE DOURO

Whether you say Duero or Douro, there is no wine story on the Iberian Peninsula that is truly complete without the mention of this river. What a behemoth!

It brings so much to the wine scene in both Portugal and Spain, with some of the most famous regions of both countries sitting along its banks. It starts way up in the mountains of the Sistema Ibérico, the mountains that form Rioja's southern wall.

Near to some of the highest peaks in this mountain range, the Picos de Urbión (2200 metres [7200 feet] above sea level), is where this river has its source. Way up here the little pools of water collect and start their long journey of over 970 kilometres (600 miles) to the Atlantic Ocean. It starts off rather dramatically, cascading down from the top of the mountains, but once it has made its way down from these towering heights, it casually meanders for a while. And here the river starts its journey across the northern plateau, covering the whole northwestern part of central Spain (excluding Galicia). This enormous plain stretches far away to the distant Cordillera Cantábrica mountains in the north and down to the Sistema

Central to the south, those mountains running along the northwestern edge of Madrid. It creates a colossal basin, angled slightly upwards, so all the water collected here flows out in all directions, and into the Duero.

On one occasion, when Amy and I were on a road trip across this area, it was super moody, the last days of autumn merging into winter. Rain is usually pretty scarce in the summer months. At this time of year, however, things are a bit different. That day, we had just driven from near Aranda del Duero and were heading west. As the road cuts in a straight line across the terrain, the river swerves from side to side, while every few kilometres there is another bridge that crosses the water as it darts either left or right. Driving through the Ribera del Duero, we marvelled at the vineyards lining its banks. In every direction one looked, the undulating, vine-covered hills rolled out of sight.

We were heading to the Rueda region to try some epic Verdejo. This region starts where the Ribera del Duero ends, as the river pours on ever westward. In Rueda it is much the same, the hills roll, rise, and dip for almost as far as the eye can see. That day in the river's basin there were massive clouds and each one that came over us deposited a sprinkle of rain before moving on across the plains, dragging their trailing grey skirts over the land as they followed the river in its march west.

The expanse of this area is remarkable. We stood atop one of these hills among endless vineyards laden with large, apple-sized river stones and the gnarly old vines that make the region famous. We were facing north, glimpsing the river below, while beyond were the mountains which, although far in the distance, still towered high.

All that water, falling from the sky. All of it flowing down into the basin, a gargantuan gutter from which the river snakes outwards to carry it far away.

This is not even half of the river's journey, though.

As it rounds the region of Rueda, the Duero continues its push towards the Portuguese border. Looming up on its northern bank, where the river rounds yet another bend, pitching northwest, the city of Toro sits upon its steep cliffs. Out here, despite all the river's water, exists some of the driest viticulture in the country and the wine style graduates from the bold, structured reds of Ribera del Duero to the keen, acidic whites of Rueda—culminating in some of the biggest reds you can find.

Out here, the produce is from a grape called Tinta de Toro. It is the same grape as Tempranillo, but the robust monsters made from these incredibly hot, dry plains are no comparison. They grow in squat little bush vines that rise barely a metre off the ground, their shoots crawling away in whatever direction they please. They are grown in this way so that the vine can create as much shelter for its precious fare as possible and also retain just a touch of moisture.

It is the common theme across this Spanish stretch of the river. The land is dry as a bone and the soils are poor and loose, meaning nearly every inch of water that does fall from the skies is swiftly deposited back into the river.

It is also thanks to these soils, which vary with every passing region, that we get the many and varying specialties of each. The clays of Ribera del Duero make it best for robust reds, the loose limestone pebbles of Rueda, great for whites, and finally the poor, sandy clay soils of Toro that dish out incredible reds with the intense heat of the area (don't get me started on soils, though—not *yet*, anyway . . .).

These arid conditions characterise the river's journey through Spain, but this soon changes, as I learned on another trip with my mate Pierre.

The plan was to hitchhike. We had made it out to the city of Toro on a bus from Madrid and we were headed for the city of Porto and beyond that, Galicia. We landed in Toro and, baking in the summer heat, stuck out the thumbs as we began to walk along the banks of the Duero. It wasn't long 'til we got our ride, a bunch of wild looking farmhands in a van that seemed one cough away from disintegration.

Somehow the van held it together and we were deposited in the city of Zamora. This is just a jump further along the river from Toro and the vibe is much the same, hot and dry, although the coming change is already making itself quietly known. Things seem just a touch greener in the distant hills.

Leaving Zamora, we crossed into the last region of the Spanish stretch, where the Duero becomes the Douro, and we were headed for more than just a change of name. After a night of camping, we were back on our feet the next morning, walking the 2 or 3 kilometres (around 1.5 miles) to Fermoselle. This is a little town that sits right on the border. The sun was baking that morning, it was going to be a hot day but there was a huge difference in the climate. Humidity.

This border region is called Arribes del Duero, "the Heights of the Duero," where two rivers, the Esla and the Duero converge. Fermoselle sits here beside the river, which traverses the bottom of a steep gorge some 100 metres (300+ feet) or so below the town's streets. Due to these gorges and the huge quantity of water that surges through the area, the climate is tropical, starkly different to the arid dry climes that lay behind us on the Duero's plains. The air is certainly heavy with humidity because I vividly recall my shirt sticking to me as I walked, my eyes on the far side of the river from the tiny town where there are some pretty spectacular views into neighbouring Portugal.

All of sudden the land starts a dramatic descent, as if Fermoselle is the topmost step of a cascading staircase. A giant's staircase it would have to be, and perhaps that was how it was formed, carved by a giant of the mountains who wanted a convenient spot from which to descend down to the ocean to wash his feet.

With the plains and the border now at our backs, we were lucky to be picked up by a French couple in their campervan and we began the winding drive down into the heart of the Douro region. The Spanish Duero River had officially become the Portuguese Douro. They carried us all the way to Pinhão and after a few days of camping along the riverside in Lamego, we made our way to Porto. To the river's end.

It is true that the humidity drops. It was especially high in that tiny border town, very different to the arid plains we had crossed to get there, but I will not say that the Douro was bone dry. The banks rise up steeply from the river, which creates a bit of a hothouse effect. The area is still relatively dry but this feature stops everything from getting completely parched. And the views on that drive were breathtaking. I would argue that the Douro region of Portugal has to be one of the most picturesque wine regions in the world. The river weaves its way through the land and the banks jut out in pyramidal columns stretching for the sky. From end to end of the region the banks of the river have been cut into ascending terraces. In a lot of cases they are the same terraces that were cut by the Romans, and they give the banks an edge like that of a serrated knife. This is made even more jagged when you see the stone that sits at the surface. It is of the most incredible schist and shale: grey and black and marbled with streaks of clay brown. The pieces of schist are like ragged plates, among which the vines are planted, looking like the grippy teeth that make the serration all the more savage, like the land might bite you.

Where things are especially dry, almost all the soil has been eroded (despite the dry summer conditions, the winters see the occasional heavy rain) and it is necessary for the farmers to spread manure and grow cover crops, which are left to rot into the surface of the ground in a desperate attempt to maintain the topsoil.

Its banks combed by thousands of hands over thousands of years, the river continues on through this winding Portuguese stretch in breathtaking fashion, its beauty continuing all the way into the bottle. Into all the many incredible bottles that are filled with so many stories, traditions, and styles which, if you're very lucky, will fill your glass too!

If you have ever sipped a glass of port you will know what I am talking about. The grapes used are extra ripened and have undergone a heavy extraction so that the wines pulsate with rich, fruity vitality. The table reds, although something of a recent addition to the region's offerings when compared to the port, are well known too. Similar to the port, they are powerful and structured. Very delicious stuff!

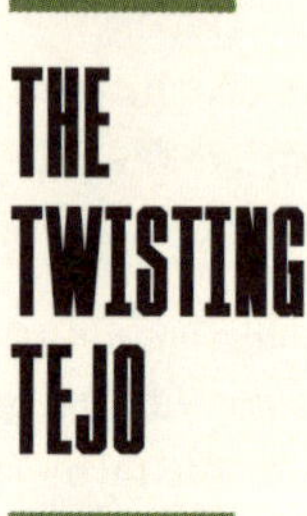

THE TWISTING TEJO

This river is a powerhouse. Pooling into the massive Sea of Straw near the city of Lisbon, the mighty Tejo first twists and turns for over 1000 kilometres (620 miles) through the centre of Spain on its way to the Atlantic coast. As you can imagine, it has a huge effect on the vast swathes of land it slices through.

And it all seems to come to a grand climax when it nears Lisbon. There is little to no notable wine production along the Spanish side of the river—but not to worry, the Portuguese make up for it. Because over the Portugal border the Tejo does something rather curious.

So, this massive deluge of water is ploughing west. It's not dead straight west but near enough. It travels across Spain in one direction and then heads across the border in the same fashion. Then, just before it is set to burst into the Atlantic, it takes a massive bend and starts off towards the south, parallel to the ocean (this is where the good stuff is). It then rounds the city of Lisbon before finally meeting the ocean.

I'm sure this is thrilling stuff for you but you're also probably thinking, why the fuck do I care?

Well, the Tejo region is especially well known for its super crunchy white wines, made from the grape Fernão Pires. All along the western coast of the Lisbon region, there is a massive impact from the ocean. It brings cool temperatures, wind, rain, even salt, which lashes the vines and seasons the wines.

But then, some 80 kilometres (50 miles) to the east, you have the Tejo River. What is interesting is that it's almost as if the two are working together to create these incredible winemaking conditions. The river is out there, doing its thing, keeping things cool and easy breezy as it trips to the sea. The ocean meanwhile pounds at the coast, its salt reaching far inland. At a certain point this is inevitably going to fizzle out. But then, just around the point where it might start to lose its power, the Tejo River is right there, backing it up. It creates this sort of bicoastal effect. The weather is cool, windy and, in effect, "coastal" all the way inwards and across the river to where the Alentejo begins (Alentejo comes from the Portuguese além do Tejo, meaning "beyond the Tejo"). The change in conditions is remarkable here, and this bicoastal effect is what appears to be behind it.

Regardless of why, the wines this phenomenon puts out are rather wicked. All this parallel activity seems to have a large-scale effect on the sandy, limestone soils, which so expertly cultivate the famed Fernão Pires.

The river also has served another function for wine, and a rather interesting one. Back in the Middle Ages, when almost all travel was incredibly slow, water was a great tool for transport. It could significantly speed up journeys, turning multi-week long excursions into trips of just a day or two. This meant that the Tejo was often used as a highway between Spain and Portugal.

Of course, times were tough and the two nations loved to fight, but still there remained a decent amount of trade between them. One of the things that was well received in Spain—and something quite a bit different to what they knew—were the wonderful wines of the Tejo. Situated along the river highway from Lisbon to the then capital, Toledo, this winemaking region was rather conveniently located. The ships started to take their wine up the river, where it was much enjoyed.

It's widely reckoned that these were some of the first wines to be exported from Portugal. Hard to tell for sure, knowing that the Romans and the Phoenicians once had a stretch of time here, but even so; these were among the first exported wines of which we have any record.

What's more, all this made the Tejo region very rich. So much so that it is believed the Tejo region was the richest in the country throughout the Middle Ages until the river started to be dammed up. Of course, a lot of big, global interests were yet in store for Portugal, so its status did not remain as such. But the region still enjoyed its time of glory, I am sure. It had its 15 minutes, at least. And there are lots of great wines continuing to pour out of this region today. So, make sure it's on your tasting wish list if you haven't tried some already.

An interesting thought occurred to me recently regarding the similarities between some of the wine lands in my home country and the Tejo region. As you may or may not know, New Zealand is pretty big on its Sauvignon Blanc. Fuck tonnes of it is grown in the Marlborough region at the top of the South Island. The majority of the good stuff is grown in two river valleys that go from southeast to northeast where they meet the Pacific Ocean, an area known as the Cook Strait. The rivers here are known as the Awatere and Wairau rivers. And their geographies are notably similar to the Tejo.

If the Southern Hemisphere is superimposed over the Northern, the land of New Zealand lies in more or less the exact same geographic location as Portugal, Spain, and France. Looking at things this way, we can see that the Tejo River is positioned in a similar position to the Wairau and Awatere rivers, flowing from the northeast towards the ocean, southeast of where it crosses the Spanish border, while in both of these locations, the soils are made up of loose alluvial soils and the area receives both decent rain and a load of sunshine.

What I am getting at here is, perhaps instead of so much Sauvignon Blanc, it's time we diversified our offering. Already, growers in NZ have been having success with Albariño/Alvarinho grapes, the Iberian import adapting well to their comparable terroir. I reckon we should throw some Fernão Pires into the mix too. Maybe even some Arinto. These are growing with native brilliance in similar conditions over here, so why not give it a go? It would be amazing to see what the New Zealand terroir would do with them. So, if there are any New Zealand–based winemakers reading this who are mad enough to take up the challenge, drop me a line. Let's get you some clones!

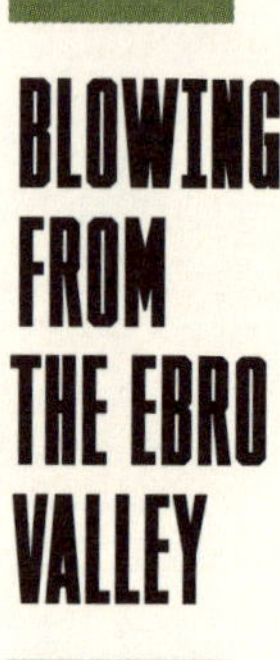

BLOWING FROM THE EBRO VALLEY

Not to be outdone, the Ebro too is one hell of a river. It starts way up in this tiny town called Fontibre in the Cordillera Cantábrica mountain ranges, separating Spain's central plateau from its northern coast. From here the Ebro begins its long journey across the north of Spain's high centre, cutting giant rifts between massive mountain ranges as it bulldozes its way to the sea. It travels nearly a thousand kilometres across Spain, making it the longest river in the country.

And wow, it sees some incredible sights on its way. The first and foremost being la Rioja, the jewel in Spain's crown. The region is built around the valley that this river created as it tumbles down from the mountains above and to the west. It is the river that stops the Cordillera Cantábrica from linking up with the Sistema Ibérico, the massive range of mountains stabbing the sky all the way down to Valencia on the coast. Either side of the river valley, mountains loom and set the scene for what is an incredible wine region.

On that same trip where Amy and I drove along the banks of the Duero, from Ribera del Duero to Rueda, we also visited La Rioja. We had been to see a producer out east, in what is known as Rioja Oriente, and had driven the length of the region, through the city of Logroño, the region's capital, where the river cuts the town in two, then carried on up to the hills north of the river, to what is known as La Rioja Alavesa. From there we descended towards the Duero, which took us through the third part of the region, La Rioja Alta.

La Rioja Alta, steep and tight, slowly progresses down to La Rioja Oriental, the region's most easterly part, where the valley, curbing round the most northern reaches of the Sistema Ibérico (the range that cuts across all the way to Valencia), widens and plateaus. The area is well known for the incredible wines it puts out, but there is a little more to it. The area also has a huge meteorological effect on a multitude of wine regions that sit beyond La Rioja to the east.

It is here where the wind known as the Cerc originates, said to generate from the cooling effects of the Ebro River on this valley. The hot air is displaced by cooler air slipping down from the mountains and this produces a current. The wind descends from the valley and across the arid plains around the city of Zaragoza. From here it continues, with the river constantly adding more to its cause, blowing all the way to the Mediterranean Sea. Its effects are said to influence wine production in a number of regions such as Navarra, Somotano, Campo de Borja, Costers del Segre, Terra Alta and more, where it brings a steady warming gust that vanquishes any humidity that has collected or drifted in from the Mediterranean coast. Humidity is a real killer, folks, bringing rot and disease, so the Cerc saves many a good batch of grapes from never making it home to our glasses.

When I spent time living in the Terra Alta region the Cerc was often a welcome change, mostly in the winter, when it would come blowing from the north, bringing with it a warming effect to loosen up the cold's grip. What I didn't know then was that I largely had the river to thank for this little boost, so a belated thanks to the Ebro, I guess!

THE WELCOME WINDS

Now we can't give so much love to the Cerc without a bit of general chat about winds. They play a massive part in the production of good grapes, so it's only fair.

We like the winds. They bring a cooling effect to some areas and a warming effect to others, each providing just what's needed. The key thing though is that, hot or cold, they bring a drying effect to the vines.

Don't you just hate humidity? It makes your hair all frizzy and oftentimes you're just sitting there, sweating through your shirt for no reason at all. Well, the vines don't like it either—although more because of that aforementioned rot and disease, which is fair. The added warmth and moisture that the humidity brings provides the perfect environment for a whole host of shithouse little bacteria and fungi, among other things, which once they spring into action can ruin the crop. Not cool.

The winds will save them though! They will whip through the area and dry everything out and keep them free from spoilage. Another reason why location is so important.

So where do the best winds come in? It's pretty fascinating how wind works. And it's really quite simple. In fact it's the same principle as what's called

Fick's law of diffusion, where something of high concentration will move to an area of low concentration, with a state of balance being the end result.

And for wind? Well, it's the flow of hot air to places where there is cold air and vice versa. But there is a problem and that is the sun (maybe not a problem, exactly—she's a sweet gal of course, but in the case of wind's never-ending battle for balance, kind of a troublemaker). The sun heats at the equator but not at the poles, so the hot air rushes from the equator up and out while cold air is likewise pulled towards it.

The coast plays a big part here too. Hot air on land caused by the sun heating it during the day is replaced by an influx of cold air from the sea. And at night it's often reversed due to the water holding onto that heat. The land then sends a jet of cold air out over the water.

So. Winds. Kinda cool, huh?

HOT PLAINS AND THE COOL NORTHERLY

Living out on the hot plains of Alentejo, in the city of Évora, we get a few scorching days. The place is famous for its oppressively hot weather, which is not shy and will reach the 40s (100s F) in midsummer. This produces some very hot and arid conditions for the winemaker. Without a little DIURNAL SHIFT, they're gonna end up with a hot mess on their hands.

But there is a saving grace. When Amy and I first moved here and were becoming used to the climate, we noticed something. Each night as the last bead of sweat drips this strong wind picks up, blowing over the plains, bringing us a much-needed respite.

Winds in Portugal are pretty common all over the place due to the fact the mighty Atlantic washes the western coast. These are your classic coastal winds and they bring a strong breeze inland too. The confusing thing about this wind out in Évora though, is that it does not come from the coast, which sits away to the west. This is a northerly gust.

It had me rather perplexed. I obviously appreciate this wind a lot. It drops temperatures at a steep angle from the high 30s around dusk to a chilly

15 degrees come sunrise. But I couldn't figure out the reason it was blowing in from the north. That is until I started learning about Katabatic winds.

Blessed with an awesome name, these winds originate on a mountain slope. During the day, the land—both the valley or plain and the mountainside—is being heated by the sun. On the mountainside there is more radiation, so the air is hot and rising. This tends to cause a current of warm air that blows up the slope. This is what they call an Anabatic wind.

At night however, things switch round. All of a sudden, the mountainside is colder—less atmosphere means heat doesn't linger. The land below is still full of heat and it's putting out warm air, which is still rising. Now a cold current develops that comes down the mountain, blowing onto the valley or plain below.

It all clicked when I read that.

The Serra de Estrela, the highest mountain range on the mainland of Portugal, sits in the centre of the country and below it to the south the sweeping plains of the Alentejo unfurl. Évora sits in the centre of these plains, which sear in the summer heat and are then cooled by this northerly breeze. Not only does the mountain range sit to the north but so does the Tejo River, which also must have some effect on the winds crossing this region at night.

Thanks to these Katabatic winds, which chill the region right down throughout the night, the grapes get a long maturation and come out bold as hell but sharp with acidity. A brilliant balance.

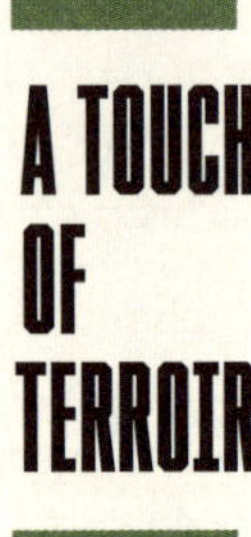

A TOUCH OF TERROIR

We have talked a lot about location, the rivers, and the winds. However, we should probably complete this image with some discussion of terroir.

Oh, that magical word, terroir (pronounced *terr-wah* if you weren't sure—so fancy and French). This is a big jam in the wine world. Everyone producing wine wants to get in their two cents' worth about their own privileged terroir and why it reigns over all others. They bang on and on and on, like a broken bloody record. It's mentioned on every label, website, or presentation about wine. It's a downright obsession!

(Also, those drinking the wine are often going to spend a long time discussing terroir as they sip.)

But perhaps rightly so. I mean, this is the whole fucking point to why wine is so special, right? Wine is a piece of time, weather, soil, sun and season all squeezed into liquid form. It truly is a way to consume a landscape or a chunk of geography as it was over that particular and ever-varying growing season.

Let me dig a little deeper.

In this world there are a lot of things that can be easily replicated. Take beer for example. I am aware there are a million types of beer. I like them a lot, but they all follow a recipe that, year after year, the makers churn out. With more or less any wheat, malt, water, and yeast, you can whip up a brew that'll quench a mighty thirst. For this reason, it is common to see on their labels, even though the beer comes from some exotic location like Mexico or Belgium, that it was actually produced just down the road from you, by whatever brewery was able to purchase the rights to the recipe. It may be super tasty, especially when the weather is hot, but it is replicable. I know there are many unique craft beers out there but for argument's sake I am oversimplifying.

And then we have wine.

Wine is a pure thing, an honest thing (at least it bloody well should be), something that has been especially crafted to express the very land on which it was grown in the most true and sincere manner. Yes, I am aware of all the big factories churning out shitty, mass produced, and heavily adulterated wine but get your mind off the bottom shelf for a minute. The whole point of wine is to produce something that is perfectly unique to your little corner of the world, a place that is like no other on the planet.

I remember the first time I saw this up close. One day, back when I was working at the vineyard near my family home in NZ, the cellar master called us in to assess how things were shaping up. Rain, hopefully the last of that summer season as the fruit was near complete ripeness, had come, and so we decided to call off any further work for the afternoon.

Sweet relief. My back was aching, having been bent over, thinning the leaves around the bunches of ripening grapes: an important measure to decrease humidity around the bunches and stop disease setting in.

The vineyard was on a steep hill with a ridge that ran down vertically through the centre of it. On either side of this ridge, the vines stretched out in adjacent rows. One row sloped down towards the east, the other headed towards the west, with the ridge pointing north (that's how it goes in the Southern Hemisphere; the sun comes from the north side).

We'd been called in to see two barrels of Chardonnay. One was from this side of the ridge, the other from the opposite. The exact same process was used to make both and the vineyards were barely a stone's throw apart. It would be easy to assume they'd taste the same, but the difference was remarkable. While one showed fresh, tropical fruity notes with a soft, slow acidity, the other was deep and stony with a grassy green, sharp vitality.

All of this difference came down to the terroir, for not even these two terroirs, a mere 50 metres (165 feet) apart, were the same. They both had slightly different soils and slightly different exposures to the sun, water, and wind. And as a result, the wines were markedly different, even on the same patch of land.

Now zoom that lens out and think about the variability that just one region has. From north to south, east to west, every corner experiences different conditions. And not only this, but the same spot experiences different conditions year after year.

Now zoom out to the country as a whole, which we compare to other countries, grunting approval and scratching our chins while swirling the wine that's in our glass.

And it's now that we see the impact of terroir. This is what makes wine so unique and each bottle so variable, yet so valuable (if of good quality). It's a little slice of when and where it was made. Never to be replicated and never seen again once the last drop slides down your gullet.

This is also why regions are defined and the lands are protected. The highest valued and most prized areas even being written into law as designated wine growing land in order to keep it as such forever. This is what they refer to as a *pago* in Spain.

So everywhere is unique, as is everything that comes from it. But so far we've talked all about what happens above the terroir's surface. Now, perhaps, it's time we look at what goes on below.

THE POOREST ARE THE RICHEST

Plants grow in the ground and vines are plants so as you can probably imagine the soils in which we grow the wine are pretty important. If you don't imagine this, well, they are. Keep up.

Soil is essential for all plant life because it is where the plant gets its nutrients and water. It all gets sucked up through the root systems and then the plant gets to work, making food with the light of the sun, photosynthesis style (mad!). This means soils that are rich in nutrients make the tastiest fruits and veggies and is why we love to see our garden soil rich and brown, that nice colour which usually comes from an abundance of organic matter, AKA rotten plant stuff: the perfect thing for healthy plants.

This is true for vines too, but it goes a little differently when we want to make wine.

The wild truth is that it's the poorest soils which produce the best wine! If you have ever seen wine grapes growing you may have noticed that they aren't sitting in that rich, fertile earth. No no, they're up on the hill, growing stoically between a load of fucking rocks. And not just rocks but sand, volcanic gravels, clay, chalk, limestone, all sorts. Anything but that good brown dirty dirt we want in our veggie patches, it seems.

So . . . why?

Well, it turns out, the healthy, nutrient-rich soil is just too much of a good thing for the grapes when trying to make quality wine. The vines tend to get a bit carried away. Like when people decide to live in holiday destinations. The good life takes over and all the important shit they're supposed to be dealing with that creates character is pushed aside, forgotten entirely. Bad news. To make good wine, and interesting dinner companions, we can't have this. We need a bit of struggle.

When grapes are living the good life, all their energy is put into growing bigger, taller, wider and they neglect to invest in future generations. They're just interested in themselves. There is an abundance of available nutrients for them to use and they get stuck into it. When times are shit, however, their focus switches to producing babies and sending them off to a (hopefully) better life. Vines are hardy little buggers. They'll put up with a lot. But what we find when we grow vines in seemingly inhospitable places is that the grapes are next level. And tough, unforgiving soils go a long way to bringing this about. The lack of available nutrients slows vines right down, limiting the rate at which they grow their vegetation; what's known as their vigour.

Another of the more important features of good vineyard soil is its water retention, or in some cases, a lack of it. As I mentioned in a previous chapter, grapes don't like wet feet (too much water and the grapes swell and pop), so the soil needs to be able to drain off. In wet areas, for example the Vinho Verde, we want things super drainy, nothing retained whatsoever. The frequent rain will supply the vine with ample water as it goes rushing by. In arid places, however, it is a little different. Due to the long hot summers a little water retention is sometimes optimal. In general, we want them dry so that the sugars concentrate in the grapes, but we also can't dry the vines out entirely. I mean, we need to keep them alive. It's a tough balance to maintain and sometimes irrigation is necessary under extra dry conditions.

For making wine, we need real high concentrations of sugar and flavour. This is the reason for siding with the poorer soils: the vines do a much better job. Winemakers will often tell you that you can't eat wine grapes because they're too strong in flavour. I call BS on that, but they are intense. They are like the fresh fruit version of a mouthful of blackberry jam. It's a lot, but it's still really tasty. When these super concentrated grapes are then squished and fermented into the wine, the result is a lot richer too. They pack a lot more complexity, flavour, tannin, the whole kit and kaboodle. And it's this that gives us a much more complete and truer expression of the tasty, tasty terroir.

I mentioned the crazy variety of different soils that are found beneath our vineyards—clay, sand, limestone, schist, and more. But before we get in too deep, here's what each will produce in the grapes that result:

- **Clay:** Makes bold muscular wines. Lots of water retention and organic matter means the wines stand strong and tense in the mouth, usually with a deep colour.
- **Limestone:** Makes wines with racy acidity that goes a long way to good ageability. The limestone retains water when it's dry but also drains well when necessary.
- **Sand:** Brings out the aromatic and elegant edge to the grape and resulting wines. Without much to cling onto here they ripen with a real fine and perfumy character, low in tannin and pale in colour.
- **Stony soils:** Granite, schist, slate, and the like mean free-draining soils that retain heat (except granite) and produce wines with big acidity. Each has its own unique mineral expression that it gives to the wines.

That's just a quick look. Of course, there are some that stand out from the bunch as a little more special . . .

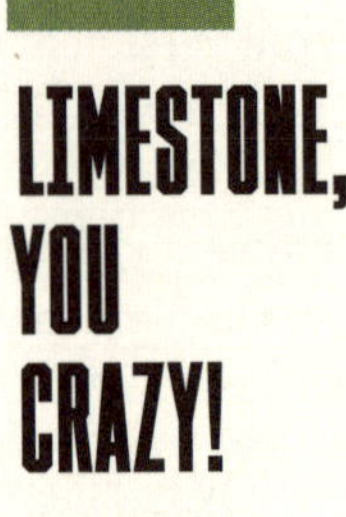

LIMESTONE, YOU CRAZY!

Within the world of geology there are a lot of fascinating rocks. Although, in the case of limestone, there is maybe a little more to it.

It appears in a number of places, including many wine regions around the world. The Champagne region is famous for it, right? There's also a lot in Iberia. Bairrada, for one, as we've already covered. The massive central region of Spain known as Castilla-La Mancha has quite a lot too, and Jerez has the famous Albariza chalk soils. In all of these places and more there is a decent amount of lime.

But did you know that a lot of this is biological? As in biological . . . rock!?

Kind of, yeah. It is a rock that has formed over millions of years from the shells and fossilised remains of sea creatures and coral. They all would have died at one point and sunk to the ground where they were covered under more fossils and sediment and compacted until—boom!—they're rocks. Some crazy stuff, huh?

This now begs the question, however . . .

If they were sea creatures (under the sea and shit), deciding to make themselves into rocks, how come they are now on land, in some cases far inland from the sea? Well, the thing is that all those places *used* to be under water, but then the earth began to shift. Somewhere around 200 million years ago Europe started to split from the Americas and, as it did so, it opened up swathes of sea and ocean, such as one called the Tethys Sea.

Then one day, 10 to 20 million years ago, the tectonic plates beneath Africa and Europe started to collide and that formed the Alps and other mountains. As these mountains were being formed, a lot of southern continental Europe rose out of the sea. Which were exactly the places where all those dead guys were hanging out. And that's why we have limestone in those places today.

Kind of mind boggling, right?

THE HIGHLAND HONEYCOMB

As I let slip in my little journey overview, I once spent a spell in the highlands. By this I mean the Terra Alta region, a little wine region in the far west of Catalunya. It's called that because it's rather high.

The whole region is this plateau that sits at the top of a mountain range. When driving from the coast, you follow this river and then the road veers off and you begin to climb. The road is pretty steep, all the way up, but when you get to the top, all of a sudden the land stretches away before you on this big sloping plain. The Terra Alta. It's a curious place for many reasons. A lot of good wine, as you can imagine, but also some rather unique soil.

Towards the end of 2019, I took a job out here in the little town of Batea. That was right before the dreaded Covid hit. The job didn't work out so well, mostly because the boss turned out to be a raving, narcissistic lunatic. No big deal. The timing could have been a little better, however. My life there started to unravel just as the world was doing the same, leaving me marooned, forced to wait out the storm. Luckily, this tiny town of around 1000 people, most of them very old, had a few good sorts (even the odd young sort, too) with whom I became well acquainted.

Batea is a crazy little town for a vinophile. Every square inch of land that surrounds the town is covered with vines for miles. The town itself is just one big winery, with near on every door hiding another winemaker's project.

You can smell it in the air too when the harvest comes. The streets are thick with that dizzying, fruity perfume that the ferments cast off as they bubble away. Suddenly, the town will have dense traffic jams on its two or three streets, too. A little different from the ordinary, however: these are made up of tractors swarming with wasps and bees which hover over the full loads of grapes in their trailers.

One of the "good sorts" I had the good fortune to befriend was Joaquim Bielsa. Joaquim and his family are behind the Bielsa Ruano Vins project. It's a relatively new project with excellent wines, but the family has been working their land for yonks. It was working with them that I got to learn about this funny substance called *panal*.

This is the name for the soil into which the vines are planted. It looks like dusty, yellowy-white clay and it is spread thick across the large *fous*, the local name for the gradually sloping terraces cut into each of the little valleys spanning this plateau. Clay is popular in vineyards; it packs in a lot of nutrients, retains a lot of water, and makes bold, muscular wines. This *panal* has a few different attributes, however. *Panal*, quite curiously, is the Catalan word for honeycomb, which gives us some idea of what's going on underground.

This whole area, they reckon, was once below the sea, and this *panal* is formed from silty, alluvial clays that are packed with chalk and lime. Gotta love them fossils. Apparently, it all fits together like a honeycomb. When compact it is hard but when the rain comes it sucks up the water like a sponge, with the excess flowing away, but which it retains long into the dry summer season.

So much so that Joaquim and his father, Augustin, would often tell me that I had to walk on the tractor tracks and not in the middle of the rows as we worked our way through. Where the tractor had passed, the soil was hard and compact, but between the rows only a thin crust had formed where the soil had dried. Underneath, it was still damp as if it had just rained.

Aided by this water retention, the vines are able to withstand long periods of drought, the time between each drop of rain sometimes spanning the full length of spring and summer.

This awesome mix of lime and clay at just the right quantities means the wines of this region—and especially Joaquim's, mostly made from Garnatxa blanca and negra—are usually lean, with prominent acidity bred from the lime, but just a bit of flesh in the middle of the body, a result of the clay's influence that gives us something truly special.

THE ROCKY STAIRWAY TO HEAVEN

So, while we're on the topic of soils, not far from the Terra Alta region in the direction of Barcelona there is another wild one. Perhaps even wilder. They call this stuff *llicorella* and it is the sacred soil of the Priorat region.

Geographically, Priorat is a funny place. It is basically just a slice of a mountain range sitting in the middle of a larger mountain range, the Sierra de Montsant, which is also another wine region called Montsant, that surrounds it on all sides. Nothing complex so far, right?

This section of the range has always been rather poor. There's fuck all here apart from steep ass mountains covered in rocks, barely a grain of good soil to be seen. There were some old monks that landed up in those hills in the 14th century to make wine, which apparently made a scene back then. They called their priory Escaladei, the "Stairway to Heaven," and supposedly cooked up some epic brews. The vibes were massive. Apart from that though, it's been pretty dead. However, in the 1970s a couple of mad winemakers decided it was a hot ticket and went for it. When they arrived, things were run by cooperatives who were dishing out liquid shit (the usual story), but these guys saw it for something else. Something about that gnarly rock and the high altitude . . .

Amy and I went tripping through those lands once upon a time. We were on a pleasure cruise from Barcelona to the Terra Alta and back. I wanted to show her where I had once spent some time living, but I was also pretty keen to get deeper into what the Priorat is doing—great wines were found, but also incredible *vi ranci*. Stay tuned.

It is an epic place, for sure. And an intense area to drive around; you can see why it has been more or less deserted throughout history. The roads are coiled like springs that swirl up to the top of each precipice to where the next village awaits. They perch precariously on the sides of the dodgiest looking rocks possible, and then to get down and onto the next town, it's another spinning rollercoaster ride along the windy path that connects them. As you drive, the neck cranes around each sweeping corner to marvel at these wild cliff-like slopes that extend near vertically into the air. Each slope that disappears into heaven, more or less, is cut into terraces to house the vines that cling on for dear life. I hope they don't have vertigo.

Winemaking and viticulture are no easy feat, but at those dizzying heights, it makes you wonder how it's even possible at all.

But we were talking about the soil, weren't we? It's fucking mad.

Here is a real stretch of the word "soil" for starters. There are some privileged patches that have something like that going on, but mostly, and more famously, we just see this incredible *llicorella*. This stuff is a form of slate that was made here some 1 to 100 million years ago. They reckon it was volcanic ash that fell into water where it turned to an ashen sort of clay. As the planet's plates shifted, this clay was then put under the immense pressure and heat necessary to metamorphose rocks and this is the result. Later on, some more tectonic activity would push these suckers up to form the mountain range and boom, wine time.

It's epic looking stuff too. Mostly a dark grey with veins of burnt orangey brown throughout, it sits in big disc-like plates, the size of saucers at its largest. Either that or it looks like crystallised sheets that crumble in geometric shapes where the erosion exposes it. And this continues all the way down through the layers and layers of "soil." The rocks break up into a sort of gravel, but it's pretty rough and rocky, with next to no organic matter therein. Supposedly the rain is able to dissolve some nutrients, just enough to sustain the vines, although as you can imagine, it's pretty hard going.

But as is the way with good wine, it likes it rough. It's the plant version of BDSM. A little weird, but tasty.

The combo of the dizzying altitude and the straight up rocks the vines are grown in fosters wines with a deep inky tone of purplish black. They are super concentrated, complex with blackberry balsamic fruit, gritty minerality, and tannin. It's heavy-duty stuff. Not for the faint of heart at all, but hella delicious if you can get into it.

Regardless, it is a true testament to the uniqueness of its terroir. A terroir warrior!

THE SHAKY ISLES

We've taken a look at soils and seen why it's the poorest that do best. This includes anything from the massive stones of the Ribera del Duero to the finest sands on the Lisbon coast. There's yet another wild one out there though, and it does something entirely different.

Volcanic soils.

Now, if you guessed that these soils came from a volcano, hey fuckin' presto. You've got it! Sometimes these are the ancient lava flows that spewed out of some angry terrestrial pimple a few million years back. Sometimes, though, they are still in the process of forming, as tectonic movement opens the land up to the hot mess below.

This occurs (and has occurred) in a number of places, but not always within the wine growing bands. These are the two latitudinal bands that encircle the earth between approximately 30 to 50 degrees north and south of the equator. It's within these bands that the best conditions for wine production are found. Now you know why they are not producing mad wines in Colombia or Norway, but I digress.

Back on the subject of those volcanoes fortuitously *within* the wine growing bands, and we find there are a couple of spots. The most interesting? Well, of course my very biased opinion leads me to say Iberia.

Not on the mainland, however, but the islands circling the top of Africa in the Atlantic Ocean, namely the Canary Islands belonging to Spain, and Madeira and the Azores belonging to Portugal. These islands were all formed from lava that spewed out of volcanic eruptions. The liquid lava would have rolled down the mountainside and, upon contact with the cooling ocean water, become solid. This activity would have continued gradually over time until the islands we know today were completely formed.

For the most part I can talk about this phenomenon in the (very distant) past tense, but more recently, a devastating volcanic eruption on Gran Canaria in 2021 saw another 43 hectares (106 acres) of land added to the island. Unfortunately, this new land will be harsh and jagged and won't be useful for a long time, if ever. Thankfully, there is much older stuff.

It presents itself in a few different forms, such as loamy soils that are rich in a stone called basalt on the island of Madeira, volcanic clays on the island of Tenerife and straight up igneous rock sands on the islands of Pico in the Azores and Lanzarote in the Canaries.

Like the land here, the wines produced from it are wild themselves. When talking about the minerality of a wine, what we are commonly referring to is how the soils impress some sort of mark upon the grapes grown herein. How they do this is still something of a mystery (science can't yet tell us), sure, but it's definitely "a thing," and volcanic soils have their own unique effect.

It's pretty fascinating actually and can make for some incredibly distinctive expressions. There is even a special term for it, known as "volcanic reduction." "Reduction" is a term that's thrown around a bit. It loosely refers to the amount of oxygen in a wine, with oxidised wine sitting at the other end of the spectrum. In truth it goes a little further than that, relating to volatile sulphur compounds that develop and show themselves in wine that doesn't receive a healthy dose of oxygen during ageing. Too much vinegar is no good, right? But too little and the "reduction" notes start to pop up and some undesirables start to raise their ugly heads. Things like egg, onions, or rubber. Not cool, mate.

Volcanic reduction has a bit of a different spin though. I should say that this isn't exclusive to volcanic zones but it is in these particular landscapes that this phenomenon seems to crop up the most. It's believed that a lack of nitrogen in the soil causes the yeasties to start putting out these volatile sulphur compounds. And they can be delicious.

It's mostly in white wines that they show up, with these crisp volcanic whites giving off smoky notes, like that of matchsticks and flinty stone. They can be somewhat intense on the first sniff or sip, almost stinging the nostrils. But as you sip it more, the phosphoric notes move into the back-seat and settle in the palate.

In red wines it's equally as fascinating but a little different, with the wine giving notes of graphite and pencil shavings. It is certainly less intense than the white wines though, where such characteristics seem to integrate deeper into the wine.

It really is bizarre on first encounter, but as you become accustomed, these brazen notes can be really fun. The potential food pairings here are worth mentioning too. Working at Restaurant SEM in Lisbon we had several dishes, especially around early spring and summer, consisting of super fresh vegetables like asparagus. And the wines from volcanic regions seemed to electrify these dishes and give them a whole other dimension; the stony, smoky notes integrating with the fresh green, vegetal flavours, combining to give the dish a lingering complexity.

One spring, Amy and I were up for a little trippin' (and, as you would imagine, some sippin'), so we made our way out to the island of Tenerife. The air was humid and clouds hung in a ring around the island's high central peak. On this trip we had the pleasure of meeting up with the producer, Borja Perez. He showed us his vineyards, which perch on the sloping banks, a steep 300 metres (980 feet) above the pounding sea. Here the soil is a rich brown clay that is filled with volcanic dust and ash.

Borja is an excellent winemaker, but he is equally skilled in viticulture. He is an expert on growing grapes in the local environment. This is the honest way too, using no chemicals, so his grapes are the truest possible embodiment of the land. As a result, his wines lean into the volcanic element—as they should, being so blessed with the volcanic soil.

After a spin around the vineyards, we headed into his little cellar to see what was in the making. It was wild tasting straight from the barrel, where the raw wine was still battling it out to find its own space and sense of calm. In these samples the smoky, burnt sulphur note leapt from the glass and threatened to singe the nose hairs. It may sound unpleasant when put into words, but it is incredible and a true expression of the land. In the bottle, when the wine is ready, the smoky gunpowder kick provides a smooth, flowing, well-integrated aspect to its profile.

The terrain may be otherworldly, but Borja Perez certainly knows how to tame this beast, his mastery made evident in some incredible wines.

THE VOLCANIC MOONSCAPE

There's volcanic and then there's Lanzarote. This place takes it to the next level. Much the scene of many trashy package deal holidays, the island doesn't always get the best wrap. It does, however, possess some of the most outlandish viticulture on the planet. This was the next stop for Amy and me as we hopped islands after Tenerife.

Lanzarote is another island that formed when lava started spewing out of the sea. It would have been a terrifying sight too. The aptly named Parque de los Volcanes and the Timanfaya National Park sit in the island's centre, offering a view to just how intense it would have been. Here layer upon layer of lava has built up across a vast inhospitable plain. The volcanoes rise up from this wasteland, awash in colours of burnt red and sulphuric yellow. The plains, however, are a dark grey-black; the sharp stone is so jagged it's almost vicious, with piercing shard-like teeth in every direction that make them impossible to traverse. One could be easily mistaken in thinking they are walking on the surface of the moon.

At the edge of this park the terrain relaxes somewhat. It's almost as barren, but the gnashing teeth recede to gravelly, sandy soils that seem to have the weight and form of popcorn. This igneous rock, formed from the dried lava, is hollow and holey, sort of like Swiss cheese. No water is retained

here, although the lava cap does appear to hold moisture in and stop it from escaping into the air. Man, how the wind whips though. There doesn't seem to be a moment where your ears are not ringing with its harsh blow.

And still, there are vines here. Suffering, just the way they like it. Or how we like it. One of the two.

As you can imagine, farming on this island is no walk in the volcanic park. Nor is grape growing. For the reasons listed, the incredibly poor soils and the relentless wind, normal grape growing is just not possible. This means some innovation has had to take place.

To get around the above issues, proving that precious wine is not just a want but an imperative, the farmers decided to dig. The majority of the volcanic activity happened around the 18th century, with the fertile soil of the preceding lands then buried deep below the lava. So, down the farmers went in their search for it, penetrating through the lava "popcorn" oils they call the *picon*. The vines were then planted at a depth of roughly a metre and a half (5 feet) below the surface to give them a head start at reaching the precious fertile soils below. Next, a small wall was constructed around the northern and eastern edges of the pit, known as a *zoco*. This protects the vines from the harsh trade winds sweeping the island.

Nowadays, almost the whole central area of the island is planted with vines, which are all sunken into their own little pits as far as the eye can see. The land here, although still rather lunar-like in parts, looks to me more like the surface of a golf ball.

Unfortunately, that's all I got to learn about the island and its grape growing. The handful of talented winemakers I reached out to were all impossible to get a hold of. (Talented) dicks! Next time though.

How much do you love a good beach day? The sun, the sea, the sand between your toes. But do you like sand in other places?

No, I am not referring to *those* places. Get your head out of the gutter. What I am getting at is, how about that sand in areas other than the beach? You know, like the desert. Perhaps more enticingly, there are a few wine regions with sandy soil and they make for some interesting terroir.

A number of pockets of sand can be found around the world in suitable locations for grape growing, including a few in (surprise) the Iberian Peninsula. They not only make good, as well as unique, conditions for growing, but they also possess a secret attribute, one that has helped them live a lot longer and in their natural state.

To begin however, let's take a closer look at these sandy plots. What do they do?

As you know, sand is pretty loose, easily dispersing into individual grains as it slides between your fingers. Being so loose, the vines have an easy time of putting down roots, which can extend to very deep places without much challenge. This makes for really healthy root systems. And this being the case, they are able to draw up those deep-dwelling minerals. Great!

The loose sandy soils also mean there is sufficient drainage, so the water doesn't hang about, allowing the grapes to get just what they need but no more. Also, great. A third benefit is the warmth trapped within the sand. It is particularly good at capturing and retaining heat, which can be helpful when things start to cool down towards the end of the year. The extra warmth the sand picks up can even extend the growing season by a bit too, so the grapes can hang in there a little longer and develop more complexity. That really is great!

But what about pest control? Well, sand actually has a remarkable advantage in the face of one very devastating problem. The antagonist of this story is Phylloxera.

Phylloxera is a nasty mite species that has wreaked havoc in the winemaking world. This little sicko likes to chew the roots of the vines. They chew them right off and the vine then dies. So sad.

It's quite a story too, how this came about. See, there was a group of scientists, Dr Fuckups and Co., we'll call them, and man, did they fuck up.

In the middle of the 19th century, they caught wind of those varieties of grapes native to the Americas across the pond. Curious, they made an expedition across to check them out. Curiouser, they decided to bring samples of those vines back with them to Europe where they figured on making some mad wines.

But as the story usually goes, curiosity killed the cat. In fact, it fucking murdered it and scattered the bloody remains in every direction imaginable. What was soon discovered was that these vines from America were infested with this special type of mite called Phylloxera.

The American vines of course knew all about it. They had come to co-exist over many years of living side by side, so the mite caused them no harm. But the European vines? Totally devastated. By the end of the 19th century Phylloxera had killed nearly half of the French vines and had caused massive devastation all across the rest of Europe and the world. The wine was gone and this caused crazy economic issues too as the commodity was now in huge deficit. Apparently, folks tried everything. Goat piss, loads of poisons, and even the burial of a live toad beneath the infected vine.

Unfortunately, and very surprisingly, it didn't work. Nothing did.

That was until two American scientists, Charles Valentine Riley and J. E. Planchon, came up with an idea. As the American vine was not affected by the mite, they figured they could graft over the European *vitis vinifera*. Finally, it seemed, they had an idea that worked. They had tested it out and the results were positive. From here, the idea spread like wildfire to save the wine industry.

But yeah, what a fucking mess.

It was this huge catastrophe that now means practically all the wine vines around the whole world are grafted onto American rootstocks. It was also this catastrophe that paved the way for the French wine revolution (stay tuned). And to top it all off, and this is a real doozy, the wines made from indigenous American grapes tasted like shit. The resulting wines were never anything special!

This, however, is where sandy soils made an interesting case. The Phylloxera never took to the sandy soils and thus the vines that were planted in these areas never succumbed.

So now we like sand as a result. Also, the wines are good too. What results are wines that have lots of crisp freshness owing to the specific environmental conditions in which they're produced. These wines are light but with great acidity and it really makes the aromatics pop. The reds are interesting too, being a lot lighter and more perfumy than most.

And there are a few regions around Spain and Portugal that are putting them out. Some to look out for are Méntrida in Spain and Colares in Portugal.

And then there's the Campos Masseira . . .

THE SUNKEN FIELDS

Lining many a coast around the world, and even in some spots way inland, where the shoreline is a very distant memory, it is possible to find loose, sandy soils. As we've already discussed, they do something rather interesting for the wine, so wine-growers make the most of them wherever possible. I have visited a number of these regions and the wines are always fascinating. There is one place that I have seen, however, that is like no other. It is on the western coast of northern Portugal, where one finds the Campos Masseira.

The reason I came to hear of these uncanny lands is thanks to a project known as Tubarão, which was created by Ricardo Garrido. Ricardo, under this label, makes some super cool wines. He produces with indigenous and sometimes quirky varieties, but underneath it all they follow the local traditions of old.

As is common in the area, part of the Vinho Verde region, the wines are often bottled with a touch of unfermented sugar and upon opening, the drinker is met with a light and rather pleasant fizz. Ricardo leans into this with some brilliant still wines and a Pet Nat (*Pétillant Naturel*) or two made with local heroes like Loureiro and Vinhão. I'd heard a little about where he grew the grapes and I was intrigued, so I decided to make the trip to find out for myself what was going down.

That morning Amy and I began high up in the Douro Valley, where autumn was well on its way. In boots and jumpers we descended from an altitude of around 500 metres (1600 feet), all the way down to the coast in the town of Póvoa de Varzim. Here the sun was blazing and it still felt as crisp and fresh as a spring morning. Ricardo met us near the golf course in his awesome little 1980s soft-top Renault, which gleamed white in the sun. He instructed us to follow him as he disappeared off down sandy, overgrown paths among a sea of vegetable patches, and we scrambled to swap our heavy autumn wear for something a little more suited to this rapid return to summer. After a few minutes of weaving, we pulled into one of the little tracks and parked up. This was where Ricardo was growing some of his grapes: on old, wily vines that climbed the banks of these so-called Campos Masseira.

But what are they? The Campos Masseira are these large, football-field sized, flat-bottomed pits that have been cut into the land all along this section of the Portuguese coast. They were first dug by a group of monks conducting their monkey business (quite often wine-oriented, it seems) in the area during the 18th century. The whole coastal area, stretching north by about 20 kilometres (12 miles) from Póvoa de Varzim and a kilometre or so inland, is as flat as a board and barely a few metres above sea level. The other handy thing about this plate is that the soils are all free-draining sand, which makes for great conditions for growing vegetables and—in this case—wine.

There is a little problem, however: the wind. It blasts the area mercilessly and threatens to uproot even the hardiest of crops. Faced with this problem, those enterprising, thirsty monks devised a solution. What if they dug down into the ground a metre or so and lowered the playing field? Over the following centuries, this became the norm in the area. The locals found it to be a fantastic solution to the problem as it not only shielded the crops from the ravaging wind but also created this cosy little microclimate for crops to grow in. Thank God, I guess.

The warming effect of this microclimate was certainly noticeable on the day of our visit too, as the temperature seemed to increase (as well as the humidity) by a degree or two as we descended into the patch where Ricardo grew his grapes. Along with them being a top spot to grow their

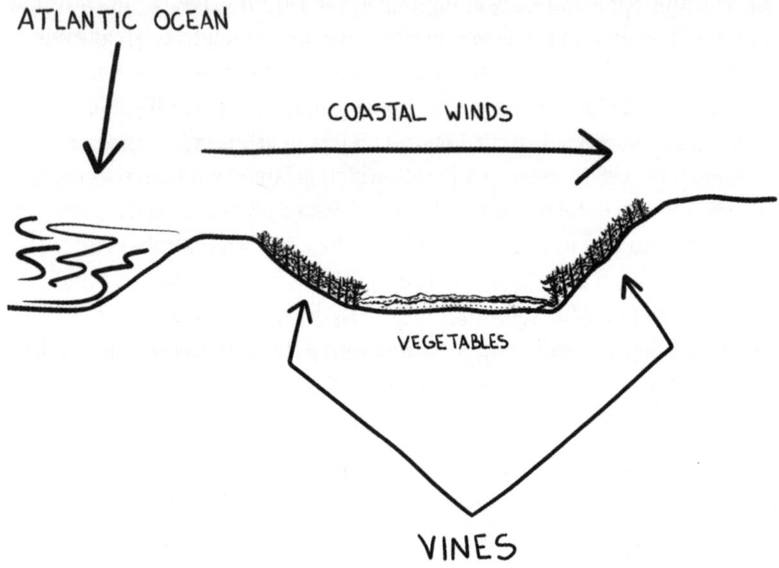

vegetables, the locals realised that the otherwise useless *valos*, or banks of the pits, would also be a superb place to grow grapevines.

And would-ya-fuckin-look-at-that, they are! With their roots in the bottom of the pits, where they can freely extend deep into the sand, the vines snake up these sloping banks from one end of the submerged field to another, creating the impression of barcodes lining each of its walls.

It was at this moment, as we discussed the incredible growing style looming above, that Ricardo popped a bottle of his exquisite Pet Nat, which glows with a reddish-golden hue and is made from the very grapes that surrounded us there.

"The local farmers, they see no value in the grapes that are grown on these *valos*," Ricardo explained. "They earn money from the vegetables they sell but see it as a wasted effort to care for the grapes that grow here."

It has since become common for the farmers to pull out these grapevines, as there is no value in keeping them now that no one is buying them. And what a shame. Because the wine was fantastic. A mix of red and white grapes, Loureiro and a touch of Vinhão, all sourced from the Campos Masseira and left to complete their ferment in the bottle to give a bit of fizz, as is the way with Pet Nats. Fragrant and floral, yet crisp and dry on the palate. It started with a fruity bloom but then ended in this mineral complexity, elevated further by the tingling bubbles that really seemed to reflect the sand that the wine was grown in.

"I want to preserve this culture by making wine from these vines," Ricardo went on. "That way, hopefully, the tradition can continue."

A DASH OF SALT

When describing wine, a lot of lofty words are thrown about. One, I am sure you have heard, is "minerality." This word refers to the stony characteristics the grapes absorb from the soil. There is no scientific proof for this, but it is generally believed that different soils create unique environments which affect the way the grapes grow and what characteristics they express. They, like you, and even me, are a product of their environment.

I'm gonna throw another word out there though. One that, although along the same vein, is a bit more out there. "Salinity."

Saline salinity. Salty ass grapes. It's a thing, it's happening. And it is quite fascinating.

As you may have guessed, this phenomenon is occurring along the coasts and so here in Iberia there is a decent amount of it. Some say it is simply the expression of a fresh acidity shining above well-ripened fruit but I reckon there is more to it than this. It occurs to some extent around the Mediterranean, although nowhere quite so much as up and down the Atlantic coast, in particular the regions of Galicia, Spain, and the Vinho Verde of Portugal. Here the wind howls and the rain clouds billow as they're swept far inland. And the wind and rain both carry with them a fair dose of salt, that is then sprinkled throughout the terrain.

Within these regions, the wine is sometimes grown right on the edge of the sea, such as in the Val do Salnés in Galicia, but the hills of the Vinho Verde region are also lined with vineyards, acting like a sort of catcher's mitt for all that oceanic intensity. The salt that is sprayed around these vineyards is duly absorbed by the soil and then by the vines themselves, eventually moving into the grapes. The varieties that are cultivated here, such as Albariño, Loureiro, or Trajadura, have evolved by the ocean. As a result, their grapes have taken on some of its properties, exhibiting a graceful saltiness.

What does this taste like in wine though?

Well, it may be a little contrary to your imagination. The word "saltiness" might make us think of potato chips and the like: things that prune the lips and parch the tongue. With wine it is a little different. It is a liquid after all, so it's hardly going to dry things out in the same way. What it does do is give this well-rounded, almost creamy texture to the wine. It's not so much a lip-smacking saltiness, nor a bitterness, which salt has in high quantities. I liken it to eating an oyster fresh from the sea. They are of course salty, but the salt here also lends itself somewhat to the creamy texture. It's some strange stuff but hey, it's tasty.

Especially in the Albariño of the Rias Baixas of Spain. This is a grape that makes plenty of fresh zingy wines but it's also a grape with some serious ageability. The purer and more refined these wines become, the more they seem to express the salty ocean. It's on the nose smelling like a fresh sea breeze or clean laundry and then in the mouth the texture is soft, rounded and precise, the acidity causing salivation and the salinity providing a texture almost like ice cream. It's really something.

And it's no wonder really.

As mentioned, I once spent a midsummer break hitchhiking with my friend Pierre. We had met up in the town of Guimareães in the north of Portugal where I had been doing a volunteer project. The goal was to explore Galicia, to see where the road took us once we put our thumbs out.

As hitchhiking often is, it was a slow start but eventually we got the rides we needed to take us to the border.

After a night of camping on the Portuguese side of the Minho River, which draws the line between the two countries, we crossed a bridge over to the other side. The morning fog was still hanging in the air as we picked up our first ride with a taciturn Spanish man, who claimed to be a hitchhiker of old, keen to repay his karma.

This brought us to the city of Vigo, from which we continued immediately walking out along the roads to carry us north. Here the coast is jagged like the claws of a bear, so a lot of time was spent zigzagging east, then north for a bit, before heading eastwards again, and so on. The trail followed along the Portuguese route of the Camino de Santiago, so there were a lot of other walkers. This also meant, however, that our attempts at hitch-hiking were met with shouts of *"Camina coño!"* (Walk, you cunt!) from passers-by.

At one point, we were approaching a bridge and the road was narrowing. Just as we were about to pull in the thumb and hold out for a safer space, this small pick-up truck careened around the corner behind us and just about crashed into the bridge in its dramatic efforts to stop.

An incredibly enthusiastic guy named Pedro leapt out to open up the back for us. We threw in our bags, careful not to put them into any of the large buckets of what appeared and smelled to be . . . sea water? And climbed in the front passenger side. The usual conversation ensued. Where were we from? What were we doing here? Where were we going? We told him we wanted to go north, somewhere, to stay by a beach, perhaps. This seemed to fit well with Pedro's plans, so off we went, barrelling along these coastal roads, making conversation with our new host.

It turned out that Pedro was in the business of worms. Yep, you read that right. He proceeded to tell us for the next hour, as we drove, all about these worms that he would routinely dive for along the coasts of Galicia.

At one point he mentioned that a quick stop was necessary. He had to drop off some worms, naturally. We pulled into a little country lane and hurtled precariously between a few houses that seemed to be built on the road (instead of the common custom, of beside it), gradually climbing until coming out on a little headland where we finally parked up. And exhaled.

Vines were growing in every direction up there, their green leaves still glistening in the sun with the morning's dew. The view stretched out away and below us, all the way down to the coast, which divided the landscape. A thick jagged line of black stone and white sand cut the land into shards of green glass, reaching out into the ocean.

Pedro disappeared at this point, leaving Pierre and me to marvel at the view. A moment passed and all of a sudden a whistle came from one of the buildings. Pedro was standing in the doorway waggling a beer. We followed him inside, into a gloomy garage. As our eyes adjusted to the light, we saw row upon row of tanks, with tubes criss-crossing and water bubbling. More fucking worms. For yet another hour, we were treated to multiple tales of worms from two or three friends of Pedro, fellow worm enthusiasts. Pictures on their phones, even.

"Mira, este era lo mas largo" (Look, this one was the biggest one).

*"Y mira, tienen luzes" (*And look, they have lights), accompanying another picture of a worm that appeared to glow in the dark.

We sipped our beers and smoked their joints and tried to convey interest with continued questioning, our Spanish too limited to be entirely convincing. Finally, after I don't know how long, the job was done, whatever the job was. The worms were worming and we were back on the road. Pedro dropped us at a supermarket, not far from the beach town of Xanxenxo. Before he left, he helpfully pointed out a place to camp just down the road and, with many *gracias* and well-wishes, we parted ways.

Pierre and I stocked up on some dinner supplies as well as some local wine for the evening. The vineyards lined the road all the way down to where the jagged black rocks that we'd seen from above marked the shoreline. The vines here were planted on high, arching pergolas—creating extra airflow as protection from the humidity. It appeared to us the vines were, as believed by the locals, growing with their roots reaching into the sea. It is quite an impressive sight, one that extends all the way along that jagged coastline, through what is known as the Rias Baixas region. The vineyards almost looked like racks of seaweed, dredged out of the ocean to dry in the sun.

Come to think of it, the wine did taste a little salty when we drank from the bottle that evening, seated as we were among the sand dunes, watching the waves. Or maybe the sea breeze was just flicking salt onto our tongues. I'm not entirely sure.

We never did figure out what the fuck was happening with those worms either.

As you may have seen before, vineyards can be hella pretty. Especially in the summer, when all is in bloom and their lil grape babies are hanging in there, ripening up real nice. But then comes the harvest, and the vines' work is done. The autumn starts to colour the leaves with all the reds and oranges it can find and the green shoots start to lignify (turn to wood) as the vine sets about sucking all the energy, in the form of sap, from its extremities back down into its trunk where it can store it over the winter months. Now the vineyard is dormant and all is silent as the vines rest and wait for spring . . .

But now too comes a special time in the vineyard calendar. Haircut time! Or, as they like to officially call it, the pruning. This is my favourite time of the year to be working the vines.

I run hot and I am not a big fan of busting my ass in the humid vineyards of spring and summer. I have done it plenty and sweated all the buckets. During the spring and summer of 2020 that I worked with Joaquim and his family in the Terra Alta, for one. Thosc long days were mostly spent head down, ass up, as we worked our way through their long rows of beautiful old bush vines, which, at the expense of my lower back, grew low along the ground. It was hot and the air was dry, but once I bent over to pick at each vine I was hit with this wave of humidity that radiated from under the leaves. So yes, a lot of sweat was sweated. I much prefer working outside when things are a touch cooler.

The dead of winter is where it's at. It is so calm, so quiet and peaceful. All is suspended, waiting for the spring. But back to the pruning.

This is the time of year where the vine is shaped for the following year. Vines are rapacious growers. Given the chance they will grow forever and produce little fruit, and none of any significant quality for our purposes. So the process of pruning is another measure that is necessary to get quality in those precious drops. This is due to the fact that the pruning sort of shocks the vine. As is similar to the poor soil trick, it conveys to the vine, "Hey, this is not a good place for you. Make babies and get them the fuck out to somewhere better where they can grow in healthy abundance!" That's the basic sentiment anyway. And then the grapevine puts all the energy it can into producing the best possible fruit (which is also yield controlled by us humans to ensure even better fruit), with the hopes that some nice bird will come along, eat the grapes, and poop the seeds out somewhere better.

All this manipulation is a little tamer than it sounds. It simply involves walking through the vineyard, assessing each vine and figuring out how you want it to be shaped for the following year before making the cuts. The cut is made in a certain place, depending on the style of pruning, so that there are a few nodes from which new shoots will burst, which is likewise where the fruit will grow. This work is slow going but rather therapeutic. And without the hot sun beating down on you, you can take all the time you need.

And that brings me to how you want the vine to be shaped. There are different pruning styles for different climates. In cooler, more humid climates the goal is to keep everything as dry as possible. Humidity brings disease, remember? The vines here are stood up straight in what is called vertical shoot position, or *espaldera* and *espaldeira*, in Spanish and Portuguese respectively. The grapes are grown along a horizontal cordon at the top of the trunk, a metre (a few feet) or so off the ground, and the shoots are held vertically with wires. The leaves are then plucked from around the fruit zone to allow for maximum airflow (facilitating dryness around the bunches). Incidentally, this was the job I was doing that day in NZ when we tasted those very different Chardonnays. This style of pruning is probably the most common you'll see all around the world these days as it produces a good result in most climates, while it's also the best suited for getting the tractor in to mechanise all the processes.

In super humid conditions, like on the Atlantic coast of Galicia in north-western Spain, they employ pergolas, these 2-metre- (6.5-foot-) tall posts with a hanging rack, way up high, that keeps the grapes as far off the ground—the most humid place—as possible. But when it's super dry? The opposite! We want the grapes to be hugging the ground. That's what you see in the beautiful old vineyards across central parts of Spain, like at Joaquim's family place in the Terra Alta, where gnarled old arms stretch only a half metre's length out of the barren earth.

This style is called the bush vine or *en vaso* (in vase) in Spanish and *poda em taça* (pruning in cup) in Portuguese. And it has been employed since the Romans brought it to Iberia after having learnt it from the Greeks themselves, a few moons ago now. With this method, the shoots burst from the tips of the vine's arms, which snake downward to run along the ground and around the trunk, thus forming a shield to protect their precious fare from the sun's unrelenting force. It may be impractical for modern, high yield vineyards but these old vines sure are pretty.

Thankfully, the artisanal viticulturists from this part of the world don't mind too much about their impracticality, nor do they care much for tractors, so still we get to see these beautiful old vineyards putting out their fruit to fill our glasses year after year.

But there is always an exception to the rule, right? Always someone, somewhere out there who harbours a little secret, a little anomaly that breaks the mould. And, when it comes to vines and how they're cultivated, this anomaly can be found on Tenerife, an island forming part of the Canary Island archipelago, which is Spanish owned but situated far down the coast of Africa, near southern Morocco.

First though, to recap the previous chapter, the normal vine is pruned each year, to encourage the growth of fruit. And how much fruit growth exactly? Usually anywhere from 5 to 20 kilograms (11 to 44 pounds). Not in Tenerife.

Grape vine production was brought to Tenerife in the 15th century. What the people found on arrival was a small volcanic island with limited space for producing both the food and the wine they needed (wine is a need too). So, innovations had to be made. And what they came up with was this style they call *trenzado*, "woven" or "plaited" in Spanish. With this style they can grow the vines and still leave plenty of space underneath for growing their food.

It was this that I wanted to see when I reached out to Jonaton Garcia of the winery Suertes del Marques. Jonaton is not only a producer of incredible wines that exhibit the brilliant terroirs and indigenous grapes of the island, but he also works to preserve this antiquated *trenzado* style of vine production.

Jonaton invited Amy and me to join a group visit to the winery one cloud-covered morning, which we gladly accepted. And it looked like we were gonna make it just fine too. That is until we arrived at the front gates at the base of his property. From this spot, I felt our tiny, rented Fiat Panda tremble as we looked upwards, necks craning to see the driveway poised at a near 50 degree angle. With first gear roaring and the transmission nearly dropping out, we drove the steep climb through the vineyards to where Jonaton was waiting to greet us. We started with a brief chat about the wine production of this area, the Valle de la Orotava, and then headed off to see the vines. And what a sight. Unlike any other I have seen.

The vines stretch outwards horizontally, arranged in a formation that looks like the teeth of a comb reaching up the hillside. As you approach, the writhing tangle of branches becomes visible through the leaves. These vines are grown from a single root—nothing strange there—but they look like a massive dreadlock and extend some 15 metres (50 feet) or more up the hill. Instead of cutting away the new growth to encourage more the following year, the vines are woven into deliberate tangles by tucking the new growth into the old each year, forming a long plait, and then bound together with a special type of string, traditionally made with the skins of bananas.

But it gets stranger still, as these 100+-year-old vines are able to produce up to 200 kilograms (440 pounds) of wine-grade grapes. It would be one thing to have vines like this that only produce low-sugar table grapes, but no, the *trenzado* grown grapes are ripe and packed with ample sugar to make a wine with 11 percent alcohol.

So how the hell does all this happen?

"Well, it's all because of the special soil we have here," said Jonaton matter-of-factly.

The soil of that part of the island is made up of volcanic clay that is rich in organic matter and, with the northern side of Tenerife being quite humid, it also gets a decent whack of water. Jonaton told me the other reason is that the vines are ungrafted, which again is thanks to the soil. Phylloxera never made it to the island of Tenerife, and we hope it stays that way, because for that reason the vines never had to be grafted onto American roots. They grow with, what is known as, Pie Franco, or French foot, and they have their original, natural roots. This means that the vine is free to produce in better harmony with its roots and is therefore more likely to grow stronger and more healthily.

The wines that result, here helped along a lot by Jonaton's very skilled hand, have incredible complexity and depth in the mouth as well as that little lick of volcanic reduction we touched upon. It's my opinion that this kind of stunning result can only be achieved through such authentic forms of viticulture.

I can't help but think there is another reason why this is possible, however. Each year at the end of the growing season, same as other vines, the vine here will pull all its energy in the form of sap down into its lignified trunk, where it can remain consolidated and protected until it is needed in the spring. But in this case, with so much vegetation and trunk, does the wild 10-metre-long (32-foot-long) dreadlock of a trunk also function as a massive battery pack, storing masses of energy ready to ripen all 200 of those kilograms? That's my suspicion anyway.

Regardless, what a mindblow. And what an anomaly!

WHY THE OLD BOYS ARE SO PRIZED

If you haven't heard already, the old boys have got it going on. Wine folks mention them at every opportunity and, like each producer's prized terroir, it's another thing that is written as many times on the label as possible. Everyone has a hard on for them. Because these vines have stood the test of time. They have been bent by the weather, shaped by steel and over generations have therefore grown strong and resilient. Is that it though? Do we just like them for their sentimental value, 'cause they've stuck around all these years?

Well, no. There's a little more going on than that.

Vines are interesting organisms. They are not designed to grow tall like a tree on their own strength. Instead, they use the support of other plants or structures to grow. Over time they go through the process of lignification, turning all of their green shoots into hard knotted, gnarly wood. It's common to see such old beasts in the gardens or scaling the sides of houses throughout the Mediterranean area. These old fellas can be hundreds of years old and they stretch to enormous lengths. The oldest grape vine we know of is the Žametovka vine growing in Maribor, Slovenia, which is already over 400 years old, although there may be older out there.

The difference here, in comparison to the vines of Tenerife, is that their fare is usually not the right sugar or flavour concentration to be useful for wine. They generally produce weaker table grapes. Nevertheless, they are incredible to see and the fruit is pretty tasty. Wine vines are a little different due to the wines' need for super intense, concentrated grapes. As we covered before, we achieve this by planting them in tough spots, pruning them back, and cutting down the yields so the grapes reach the desired levels.

What I am getting at, though, is that there is little to see above the surface. This is where the old vines have something special. A lot of the vines' energy over the years, while not producing fruit, is invested below the soil, in the complex and far-reaching root systems. Especially in areas of low water retention (loose soils like sand, or up on the hillside) where roots have grown to reach great depths to pull up water and minerals necessary to nourish the plant. While most of the root systems are usually found in the top metre (3+ feet) of topsoil, the full extent of the system can reach as far as 9 metres (nearly 30 feet) below the surface! This kind of root length pulls up a whole treasure trove of minerals and nutrients, not to mention water, to sustain the production of new growth and fruit up above.

Are all these additional nutrients and minerals the reason for the added complexity and better balance in wines produced from these old folks? Because that is certainly the result. If you look at the two sides of the ground's surface like a balancing scale, the young vine will have a lot of growth above and comparatively little below. The wines from the young vines are punchy and unsettled, too. Overblown acids or intoxicatingly perfumy fruit that goes off like a firecracker in the mouth and then fades away in a hurry. (*Cowboy natty producers look around guiltily.*)

And then the old vine. There is a lot more balance between the growth above and that below the soil than there is with the young vine—often the same (if not more) mass can be found beneath its surface. The wines produced from older vines show a lot more harmony, too, striking balance between the tannins, acids, and fruity bits. There is, as well, much more complexity to them, with their grapes containing a much higher concentration of minerals.

Is this just a coincidence and I am getting all too visual about it? It's been known to happen. But the wines are certainly in my favour.

So yeah, these old boys grow slow and put out better fruit. Unfortunately, a lot less fruit than the younger boys do, so producers who are gunning for big volume and higher bottom lines usually rip them up and replant. In these circumstances, irrigation methods are often employed to increase the rate of growth, which stunts the root systems. With ample water available, they grow their roots just below the surface, instead of way down deep in a desperate search. The wines never shape up substantively as a result, but hey, they produce quantity. Then, when the vines start to slow down, they get ripped out again. Rinse, repeat.

'Tis sad and it is good for nothing other than the profits. We shall talk more on this later when I get to regenerative viticulture.

Back to the old vines, though. It's not just growing deep roots that makes them so special. See, these old vines have weathered the storm, so to speak. Literally, in fact. Over the many years and yes, sometimes we are talking a century or more, these vines have seen it all, from droughts to floods, under overcast skies and blazing sun. Through this they have come to adjust and adapt to the unique environments in which they find themselves. In essence, these vines understand the terroir and know just how to express it best.

Better wines with greater complexity and precision in their characteristics that come from happier vines are truer to the land and terroir. It's the happy ones that maintain the health of the soil too. Not just sucking out what they need before getting ripped out themselves, these old vines give back. It's good stuff—good for the earth and good for the taste buds. Get in my glass!

Patches of old vines can as yet be found within many of your classic European wine regions in the Old World. Usually, they reside more comfortably where full exploitation is too challenging: for example, where the terrain is too rugged for tractors to pass. When found in famous regions, like the

Douro, it is because a fierce caretaker meticulously protects and sustains their growth. Artisanal producers will often have a patch or two of old vines at their disposal as it is widely known that they produce the goods. The good goods. Read the labels and you'll see.

A quick note for anyone confused by this, the Old World is the general term used in the wine world for anywhere that winemaking has been a staple since the beginning of time. This includes Europe, parts of North Africa, the Middle East, and Central Asia. Anywhere considered to be the New World, chances are that winemaking arrived on a ship not too long ago. This includes the Americas, Australia, New Zealand, and South Africa.

In the so-called New World they are less common for obvious regions. But on occasion you will find some old beauties out there, still hard at work. Safe from Phylloxera and its far-reaching damage, the sandy soils of the Barossa Valley in South Australia are said to be home to some of the world's oldest wine producing vines, planted by the first colonial winemakers 200 or 300 hundred years ago. Mexico is also an interesting case study. Mexican wine production is not often talked about but they have a few choice areas, such as the Valle de Guadalupe, where wine production was introduced by the first Spanish missionaries, some 400 years ago, with a lot of ancient varieties and old vines still being found in nearby spots today.

In any case, my money's on slow and steady for the win.

Thankfully, the concept of old vines is rather common, especially in Europe. I mean, it's flippin' incredible, these gnarly old beauties, standing strong for a hundred years or more, but yeah, it's still widely seen (where they have been protected, that is). In Portugal too, you often find it written on the labels. *Vinhas velhas* is the term in Portuguese, translating to "old ass vines," or thereabouts. But the meaning is a little different here.

Being a small country that never saw the big markets pulling at their coat tails (except perhaps for Port, but that is a part of this story too), the Portuguese producers sat back with their feet up as this globalised market developed on other shores. Meanwhile, they grew their grapes and made their wine, in the same way as they had always done. Why wouldn't they? And as a result, what counts as tradition here is a big old, beautiful mix.

For centuries, probably longer, the wines of Portugal have been made with a wide array of varieties. Currently, there are said to be over 250 commonly used, indigenous varieties! When the term "*vinhas velhas*" is used it means that the vines have been interplanted with as many varieties as those working them could get their hands on. There are a large number that are easily identifiable, yet it's often that even the winemakers don't know the full extent.

This has long since been the traditional way. The vines are planted with huge diversity and then harvested all together into big, delicious field blends. One reason this came about was security. With monoculture, if you have a problem with disease, the whole crop is doomed. That's why we're one beetle's fart away from life without bananas (the Cavendish variety at least—look it up! Or wait for my next book, *A Complete Guide to Bananas*).

By mixing and matching the selection of varieties in the vineyard, the impact of a challenging factor (water supply, humidity or heat levels, etc.) is greatly lessened, limited to affecting maybe one plant or only one of the many varieties. This means, there will always be wine!

But there is still a little more to it. This practice contributes to the prevention of things like soil degradation, which takes place due to the vast replication of exactly the same needs, season after season, year upon year, from just the one patch of soil (as is the case with monoculture farming) and, also, the general loss of biodiversity that keeps the whole ecosystem ticking by in good health. So variation is not only healthy but, as I mentioned, super tasty.

With *vinhas velhas* everything is harvested together to make wines that show amazing complexity and are as true to the terroir as you can get. This applies to red wines and whites alike. There is even the in-between too. It can be common to see the word "*palhete*" written on Portuguese labels. This is the term for a complete field blend of everything there was, red or white, thrown into the ferment together. The wines are light, green and springy with sharp acidities, bouncy fruit, and dusty tannins, best served chilled.

The wines are amazing. Although the vines themselves are truly fascinating. In my experience, nowhere more so than in the Serra de São Mamede. This is a gorgeous mountain region in Alentejo. Inland and up a bit from Lisbon, it sits hard up against the Spanish border. They lump this little area in under the overarching distinction of Alentejo wine, but it is so much more. The soils in this range are laden with granite and the air is much fresher than down on the lowlands, with altitudes reaching 700 metres (2300 feet) of elevation. DIURNAL SHIFT! The wines produced here are deep and complex, especially the whites, and the vines are old as fuck.

When my mother was visiting, we went on a trip to see the project of one João Afonso: Cabeças do Reguengo. The winery is located on the western side of the mountain range and these guys turf out some bangers—again, especially the white wines. There are a number of vineyards owned by the winery but much of what they work with comes from independent growers with whom they collaborate. I was keen to see some of these old vines so I asked João if it would be possible.

"Just follow this path here till you get to the gate," he instructed. "The senhora Eugenia will be there. She will show you where to go."

We followed the path down as instructed and sure enough, Eugenia, the owner, was there. As if she always had been. She opened the makeshift gate and led us down the back side of her property between the barking dogs. There we found the vines, and like none other I'd seen before.

The twisted, gnarled arms of each plant were splayed out in all directions, often propped up with old bricks or stumps of wood. There were no rows or organisation to them either; they seemingly grew wherever they felt best and all blended in with olive trees and pomegranates. The season was shifting into autumn at this stage and each vine was contributing to a myriad of colours. From the usual greens to bright yellows, there were scarlet hues and burnt magentas, highlighting the large mix of different varieties (of which there were over 15) as each exhibited their preparedness for winter through these differing phases.

"How long have the vines been here?" I asked.

"I have lived here all my life. They have been here as long as I have," Eugenia told me. "My father was born in 1906 and they were already here then too."

Such stunning wine heritage is a true pleasure to come across on trips like this. We just have to keep filling our glasses with it so that people like João Afonso and all the many producers he works with (and beyond) can continue to protect it.

The world has got pretty wrapped up in the whole natural wine thing. It comes from a good place. Or at least among those who understand it's not just a method for making wild tasting, disappointing wines. Hmm, I guess I shouldn't say that.

What I am trying to say here is that natural wine, at its outset, was a movement designed to produce wines free from all the chemicals that are ruining this planet. Somewhere along the way this message has got mixed up with an image of wacky "wines" and people seem more concerned about the flavours than that original message. Things, however, seem to be coming full circle again. What I mean by that is, the natural wine scene is now reverting back to the classic wine styles of old but now with better and cleaner methods. A much-needed support for our poor, suffering planet.

I am sure you have wondered, though: What is the real effect of all of this and what are these methods that are going to (hopefully) save us all? Well, I have anyway. But first, to understand all that, we have to go back a bit.

Back in the day all wine was natural, right? That is before we figured out how to make all these nasty chemicals. Wine used to be made without any additions or -cides in the vineyard. It wasn't until the Second World War that this all began. Europe, and many other parts of the world, were in a sorry state come the late 1940s, once all the dust had settled. There were a lot of men dead and gone yet still a lot of hungry mouths. Thirsty ones too. Luckily enough, leading up to the war, as well as during and after it, a lot of research was done; plenty for very sinister reasons, with science having been heavily weaponised, but some had other applications. Insecticides, fungicides and herbicides and all manner of other useful but generally horrible -cides were now available to the market—and just at the right time too.

Work in a vineyard is seriously labour intensive. It is said that roughly one man working full time is necessary for every 5 hectares (12 acres)—although that is with the use of a tractor. Without one it may be as high as one per hectare, which is how things were post-WW2. But then, all of a sudden, the labour market was decimated to next to nothing. Just as well then, that all these sprays for the vineyards came along, which removed, as they do, the need for a load of that labour, allowing food and wine production to continue without too much further upset.

And this became the industry standard. Spray the living fuck out of everything and hey presto, a perfect crop! All this at no cost to the land too, right? RIGHT!?

Wrong! Just like with cigarette smoking, there came a time when we discovered it wasn't as sexy as all the adverts said. Simple spraying, as it turns out, sort of, *kind of*, completely fucks the ecosystem. Indeed, it came to light that while we were spraying the living fuck out of everything, we were, in fact, spraying the living fuck out of everything.

These sprays get into the plants, the soils, the water, and everything in and around the land. Oh yeah, and also, anything that consumes what comes from the land, which is us. It has caused mass extinctions of insects, the ones that keep our world clean, as well as on a microscopic level. Even the microbes are getting screwed. No one is safe. These sprays effectively strip the land of nutrients, which creates the need for fertilisers, which further deplete the land, turning it all into a vicious cycle and, unchecked, triggering a downward spiral into a barren hellscape (too much?).

Miguel Morais of Quinta da Costa do Pinhão further illustrated a point one day when we were talking about herbicides on a visit to his—gorgeous, by the way—property in the Douro Valley.

"We take this poison and we put it on our plants. But it doesn't kill every single type of plant. Meaning the one that gets away then grows like crazy, covering everything. Then the land requires *another* herbicide to take that plant out, which then requires another one and then even more to take the *next* plant out, and so on."

Vicious cycle, in short.

"We find that if we just leave everything in harmony instead, nature keeps it all in check and we have little excess in terms of weed growth."

Back to the microbes though. These guys are getting killed by all this spraying too, and they are essential for healthy soil. Microbes create a healthy layer of topsoil: where everything is decomposing and recycling itself back into the wider system of living organisms. In a healthy system, this microbe level goes right down deep, creating lots of healthy space for the plants to grow their roots and take up nutrients. Furthermore, and most importantly, these healthy layers of topsoil trap carbon! The deeper the microbes are working, the more carbon is sequestered from the atmosphere and trapped below the surface.

The use of all these -cides however, kills microbes en masse, which in turn destroys the layers of topsoil right the way down to a thin little band on the surface, and the carbon within the soil is puffed out into the atmosphere—the cause of all this here climate change. To spit some facts, it is said that the soil in the United States alone could have the potential to pull down 250 million metric tonnes (276 million US tons) of carbon dioxide and other greenhouse gases each year. As of 2022, the whole world emits 37.49 billion metric tonnes of carbon dioxide per year. Spread all around the world, this sort of in-built protection for the soils could put a decent dent in this massive existential problem the world is facing.

Instead, the world continues to spray, the carbon continues to leak, the insects, microbes and more are dying and even us people are getting sick from the chemicals rotting our guts and riddling us with cancer.

I am sad to say that vineyards are some of the worst polluters too. Grapes are a very sensitive fruit to produce, especially when striving to obtain the high-quality levels we do for wine production, and we consume a lot of wine. Needless to say, it requires a lot of spray to produce a clean crop at scale. The more humid and cool the environment, the more that is amplified yet again.

Filipa Silva, Miguel's partner who also does wonderful things at Quinta da Costa do Pinhão, once had a few facts to share. In comparison to a tonne of corn, a tonne of grapes requires on average way more chemicals. Where the corn requires 40 kilograms (88 pounds) of agrochemicals to produce, grapes require up to 100 kilograms (220 pounds). Grapes also require around six times the amount of fuel, consumed by the tractors, than corn to produce a clean crop. So grape growing can be pretty nasty, which is sad to hear.

But is there any solution?

Well, of course. Drink clean. There was a time before any of this was necessary to produce a glass of wine and we were doing just fine. So, can we go back? How do we go back? Let's have a look at a few of the better farming styles which could hopefully help us reverse some of this damage.

Organic Viticulture

The first rung in the ladder of clean agriculture and, more relevantly, viticulture is organics. This is basically the removal of anything that has been synthesised. All the -cides are out but there is still a lot of spraying going on. Now it is with only organic substances, which is a step in the right direction. These are basically raw elements so things like copper, calcium, and sulphur are used on the vines.

And it is wondrous how life returns/remains as a result. A conventional vineyard, soaked with sprays, is pretty much bare of any life (other than the vines). No grass, no plants, and no insects, which are, in most cases, pretty damn useful around a vineyard. But the organic vineyards are teeming with life.

The sprays that are used, the organic substances, aren't out to kill all these vineyard friends. They aren't completely harm-free though and should be used with moderation. Unfortunately, "organic" written on the label doesn't automatically mean that everything is perfect. There is still a window of opportunity open to soil degradation. As with anything that you add to the soil, too much of it will cause an imbalance, which will leach nutrients and affect microbial life too. Organic is good, it is a much healthier way to produce our grapes, but there is better.

Biodynamic Viticulture

This is a fascinating philosophy. The whole idea sits in a bit of a spectrum. It starts with a few sound, commonly used little techniques for improving one's land, and then it can go right out to the wild and witchy. This philosophy is based on the moon and how it moves, with crops being planted, harvested, and intervened upon according to cycles based around lunar movement. On a macro level, it treats the land as a single organism and seeks to create balance within it. If there is disease in one place there must be an imbalance in another. So, farmers will use methods, plants or otherwise (but always natural remedies), found within the ecosystem to counteract that imbalance and put things back on the right track.

The horn thing is pretty nifty too. Maybe you've seen something about this before. Maybe you wonder what the fuck I'm talking about. It's an interesting trick from the biodynamic handbook. What they do is dig a pit (this has to be done on the right day in the lunar calendar) and they fill this pit with a load of hollow cows' horns that have been painstakingly filled with manure. They then wait a few lunar cycles before digging them up.

During that time, the microbes in the soil have been getting stuck into the manure. They have effectively digested all the manure in the horns. Not only this, but they have conditioned the now digested manure to be harmonious with the land. To spray or dump straight manure on a patch of land will do some good and give the plant some of what it needs, maybe, but this approach is more likely to flood the soil with nutrients, particularly nitrogen, which will cause a massive imbalance. Basically, it'd be like poisoning yourself with medicine.

Not this stuff from the horns, though. Because it has been digested and assimilated with the microbial make-up of the land, it is a ready source of nutrients and in a much healthier quantity to not overpower the environment. The manure is then diluted with water to make a sprayable liquid (a rather smelly one, I'm sure). When the farmer sprays it onto the vines it provides the right amounts of everything the vines need to be healthy for the next year. Pretty neat.

A lot of viticulturists take leaves, here and there, out of the biodynamic handbook, so it is interesting to hear what some take to be useful for their particular patch of land. On a trip out to the Sierra de Gredos one time, we got to talking about biodynamics with Paolo Armando, who is behind the very delicious project Ca Di' Mat.

"I am not a full biodynamic practitioner," he stated. "There are some really interesting points to biodynamics which we use, although not all of them work with our philosophy." He started to divulge a few of them and how the lunar cycle impacts them. There was one that struck me as particularly interesting, however.

"We only prune the vines when the moon is descending and not when it is ascending. If you do the pruning when the moon is ascending, just like with the ocean's tides, the liquid within the plant is pulled up. So, if we make a cut at that time the wound we have just made will begin to bleed with sap which will then be lost from the vine."

As we know, the sap, which during the winter is stored within the trunk, is the plant's energy source, like bees with their honey, and they use that stored energy to propel their growth once the spring arrives.

"If instead, we prune when the moon is on the decline, just like the ocean's tides, the sap within the plant will be down low and the wounds will not bleed out their precious sap. Then they'll have plenty of the energy they need when the growing season returns."

Regenerative Viticulture

At the top of the pyramid of clean practices is where the agricultural style known as "regenerative" would sit. This is a philosophy that is a little different to the rest, while still involving a mix of some of the same methodologies as those before. Regenerative agriculture takes a much straighter shot at the root of the problem—both on the micro level and the macro.

So, we talked about soil imbalance causing leaching and killing off the microbes, shrinking the healthy topsoil layer down to next to nothing, in turn filling our atmosphere with carbon, all of which should be locked under the surface, right? Right.

Well, regenerative agriculture (and viticulture) is the practice that addresses that very problem as its main focus. Currently the way that food is produced in the Western world is said to be eroding the soils at a rate that is 10 to 100 times higher than the soil is forming. This quite clearly shows that soils are not an inexhaustible resource. It ain't just fucking dirt, bro! The term regenerative means to revive or give new life to something. And it is the soils that they are looking to regenerate. In regenerative farming, we want the topsoil level to go as deep as possible, with as many healthy microbes down there as possible to trap more carbon. Plus, this not only traps carbon but makes for the healthiest of soils in which to grow crops. It's a real win-win.

How do they go about it though? Well, the main tools are animals and plants. Which seems a little vague, I imagine. We will continue to expand about plants, specifically regarding cover crops, in the next chapter. For now, I'll talk a bit more about the animals' role.

Animals are essential in the regenerative agriculture arsenal. The animals I am talking about are the usual farm crowd—chickens, ducks, geese, sheep, cows, horses, pigs, the occasional donkey. The whole gang. These guys move through their patch of land and eat all the grass and weeds, which is good! More importantly though, they shit and stamp around in it. In fact, they stamp around that whole patch of land with their little hooves, trotters, webbed feet, or whatever it is they possess. As they do so, they open up the land, put more nutrients into it and allow for more air flow down there. Repeating this process in a cycle—letting the vegetation grow, then cutting it back with the help of animals—will eventually see that top cap of soil regenerate.

I'll go into the right vegetation for the job, but it doesn't always need to be something specific. Simply letting the grass grow and hacking it back so that it rots into the soil will go a long way to replenishing and nourishing it.

No-tilling is another technique. This can lead to another heated debate among producers (be warned): those who till versus those who do not. When the soil is ploughed it actually opens it up to the elements, which then work to strip the soil of all its goodness. And this is the big argument for not tilling. Those who practise it want to maintain all the good gunk they've built up down there under the soil. Others see it differently and feel the soil benefits from a bit of breathing every once in a while (it does look kind of cool when they get out there with the horse and plough, too, but that's neither here nor there).

I have heard both sides of the story from a few different people, each side with pretty convincing arguments. What it seems to really come down to, however, is how well each person knows and understands the individual needs of their patch of land—each patch, as we know, being very different.

Regardless of who is right or wrong with this one, it makes for some interesting conversation, which has often allowed me, someone with zero understanding of whichever particular bit of land is in discussion, to gain some massive insight into a producer's philosophies and methodologies.

These are only a few of the techniques used to make the soil better, which in turn helps the entire ecosystem. It's interesting and highly logical stuff, while it doesn't half show how fucked up the way most things are normally done is.

The unfortunate truth is that we aren't supposed to be producing this much wine, and that is evidenced by the way that everything is exploited for maximum production. Same as what goes for eating ripe tomatoes in winter or mangoes in the Arctic Circle. So, these methods of production that look at each plot of land more holistically, taking what they can as opposed to rinsing it for all it's worth, are what's going to provide for us better in the future.

It may come at more cost to purchase these nice, responsibly produced wines, unfortunately, but look at it as an environmental tax. Governments worldwide seem to be doing as little as possible, at the massive corporations' behest, to enact one themselves. This is one way in which you can help.

So, I'll say it again. Drink clean wine!

And now, if you're drinking massive amounts of delicious wine all the time, just think how much good you're doing for the planet, says Adam internally, in an incredibly hopeful tone.

Not only are they useful tools for us, but plants can help other plants. Who would have thought?

What we're talking about here is cover cropping, where farmers plant different types of vegetation in the land after a cash crop to replenish nutrients and revive soil health. In the case of viticulture, this takes place during the spring, when water is most abundant. This measure can be especially necessary in areas where soils are incredibly poor. The vines may like it rough, but there still need to be some available nutrients for them to absorb. For that reason, within viticulture, this technique is becoming continually more prevalent. By planting something up on top and then cutting it as the summer starts, leaving it there to rot, we can build a bit of a topsoil layer, making the whole system just a smidge healthier. This topsoil layer, hopefully now getting deeper, is going to add a little water retention to the mix, something which is also rather useful considering these poor soils are often in very dry areas.

The addition of these crops also brings in the bugs! And the more diversity of plants and flowers, the more there will be. For grape growing there can be a lot of bad boys in the insect world. For example, wasps (as if they aren't always) can be real dicks. They do things like popping the berry to nibble at the sugar, which will then start to rot, potentially spoiling the whole bunch. There are also other buggers, like leaf-roller caterpillars, that bore into the branches, eventually killing the vine, as well as many other miniature assholes. There are, however, the good guys and they have to be celebrated as well as supported. These are things like bees, for what I hope are obvious reasons, but also because they will kill off the wasps. Ladybugs are real saviours too, and of course, everyone's favourite, spiders. I am sure there are many other beneficial bugs and if any are reading this, I am sorry for not mentioning you. You've always got to help your beneficial bug friends, though. I always say thanks when I see them around the vineyard.

Regarding those plants that do an exceptional job of supporting their local ecosystems, there are a number that stand out from the bunch. Clover, for one (great gal, clover), provides abundant fertiliser, but its most important attribute is that of fixing nitrogen under the soil. This is often the biggest benefit of cover crops: nitrogen is everywhere in the atmosphere but not always bioavailable, that is, in a form that the plants can readily absorb. The vines need it and yet often can't get it, so it's up to plants like clover to do the deed and convert it. Legumes too are highly useful for their nitrogen fixing abilities and they also like to grow deep, rather bulbous roots, which free up nutrients, as well as space, in the soil below. As a result, it's common to see peas or broad beans filling the rows between the vines. Mustard is another that's helpful to the vineyard, and then a whole host of other indigenous plants that are native to each region, uniquely able to nourish the soil.

Then there are other heroes, like comfrey and nettles. These are useful in a slightly different way. Yes, they can be used within the same methods as above but there is even more that can be done with them. And that is tea.

Well, it's sort of like tea. Nothing like the nice herbal infusion one makes to cosy up next to the fire, no, it's a little more stinky than that. The method goes that you let the comfrey, nettles, and whatever else grow. Both of these plants grow rapidly and produce a lot of leafy vegetation. Once grown, they can then be cut and left to steep in water for a few weeks. This process brings about a bit of fermentation which breaks down the plants a little as well as increasing the microbial value of the liquid. Once ready, this liquid can then be sprayed onto the vines to give them a boost. If you're really up for it you can even stir in a bit of shit for a stronger brew. Better not use your own, I reckon. Preferable would be that of sheep, horses, or cows but hey, it's your world, buddy. Live it! Regardless, it's gonna be a pungent brew—similar to the one made in the cow horns—that as a result will nourish the fuck out of those vines. We're talking heaps of nitrogen, phosphorus, potassium, and much more. All of it is so disgustingly delicious.

I once met a guy at a wine fair in Lisbon where I was busy sippin'. His name was Alex and his partner Maria are the pair behind the project Punta de Flecha. They are doing something pretty cool, so of course I had to make the trip.

Their project is a daring one and rather exciting, rooted in the vineyards lying hard up against the southwestern city limits of Madrid. Amy and I were on a mission to explore the plains and peaks surrounding the city and knew it would be essential to visit Alex.

As we pulled off the motorway heading directly towards the heart of Madrid city, we soon found ourselves on a wild dirt road that bumped and rolled itself towards the town of El Álamo. We found Alex waiting at the doors to a massive old co-op in the town centre. Built in the 1960s, it had recently been vacated and Alex, his project growing, was able to use the space. This area was once well known for the production of wine, especially rosés, but in recent times the ever-encroaching city limits and the profitable appeal of cereal production over wine had sent the local industry into decline. That's why Alex, his project producing around 10,000 bottles, is free to make his wine in a winery equipped to produce multi-millions.

After a quick "hello" and some "great to see you agains" we leapt into his truck and began the drive out of town to see the vines. It was a beautiful clear afternoon and the sun was starting to get low in the west, giving the landscape a golden glow.

"All of this used to be vineyards," Alex gestured to the wide, recently ploughed plains stretching in all directions. "Now there are only a few of us still growing grapes."

Once among the vines, we pulled onto a little track that led to a small shed, shaded by an old pear tree. We parked up and began to survey the vines. The land was flat as a board and extended far to every horizon. To the northeast, we could see the haze above the city of Madrid, and straight north, the mountains where the Sierra de Gredos is located. Otherwise plains as far as we could see. Most curious though, in this landlocked stretch of country, is that all of a sudden it seemed we were at the beach.

The lands of this area, which sits at the border between the Denominations of Madrid and Méntrida, are made up of these granitic sands that glint and gleam where the occasional quartz crystal picks up the light. And from these sands, the old vines that Alex meticulously cares for twist upwards with short, bulbous arms, their broad trunks bulging out of the soil, barely reaching 30 centimetres (12 inches) off the ground. These are old vines of Garnacha and Malvar, a little-known local variety, and they had been growing in the spot for the better part of a century before coming into Alex's care. They are works of art, showing the constant struggle between nature's vigour and humans' ever-restricting hands.

We got talking about the vines that, with help from the sandy soils, produce aromatic whites and light-coloured yet intense reds (hence the area's reputation for rosé). The subject at the forefront of my mind then quickly emerged: herbal teas. These sands, although dazzling in the light, are very poor in nutrients, giving very little if anything to the vines, even with their wizened roots reaching metres under the ground. A little help is graciously accepted.

"All of this land here," gesturing to his vineyards and beyond, "is a protected nature reserve and over there is where the protected forests begin," Alex informed us as he pointed towards some trees that lined the edge of a stretch of the plain a kilometre-or-so beyond where we were standing. "We go foraging out there to collect the herbs and plants that we need. More or less everything we need grows up there naturally."

"So, what kind of things are you putting on the vines?" I asked.

"A range of different things. Each plant is able to provide a different remedy to whatever issue we're faced with. Luckily, out here it is very hot and dry, so we don't have to intervene too much during the growing season. The sandy soils help us a lot too.

"Sometimes we have to provide a little help to the vines though and we do that with either ferments, where we leave certain herbs in water for a while to decompose into the liquid, or actual teas where we boil the plants in water before spraying them onto the vines," he explained.

"And what are these plants that you're using?"

"We pick a lot of calendula. That helps us to keep any unwanted insects at bay. Thyme is useful in that regard too. Aloe vera does the same but also can deter the birds. Sometimes, when it's really hot, we use a blend of chamomile and valerian that we spray onto the vines to release the heat and lower the temperature of the plant.

"Another one we use is horsetail. That helps us with any fungal infections threatening the vines, while nettles are useful for limiting any scarring we cause during the winter prune."

It was pretty mindblowing to learn that these common plants, or weeds for the most part, could have so many uses. I asked him how he came to know all this.

"I started my wine education in the conventional setting, but the use of these harsh chemicals never made sense to me. For every imbalance in nature, there is always something natural to counter it. I started to research the plants of our area and came across all of their ancient uses, the way folks were doing it before the chemicals came in and made it all 'so easy.' From there, I started to test them, they're growing wild out there in the woods so I had nothing to lose. Not exactly a costly experiment. But they have been working and we've managed to obtain a beautiful harmony in our vineyards, which are seemingly healthier and healthier every year."

Once back in the winery with the sampling underway, it felt as though you could taste that harmony too. The wines were full of unique character and they seemed to have their own natural balance that, with Alex's gentle hand, had been carried from the vineyard and into the bottle. The wines are fantastic and the area remarkable for super interesting viticulture. Alex is working hard to keep that culture alive despite the challenges. I am confident, due to the quality and uniqueness of his wines, that he will soon be very well known for what he does and that he will be able to continue his excellent work.

This area where Alex grows his grapes and gathers his herbs on the edge of Madrid's city limits is thankfully a protected green space—and will hopefully remain so. The family of otters that ran across the dirt track in front of us as we left the vineyards certainly agree too. A piece of paradise preserved. With this protection there's hope that the beautiful old vines Alex so lovingly cares for will be around for a good while to come.

There was another trick I once came across which I thought was neat. It came about when I was working at Restaurant SEM in Lisbon. One of our favourite winemakers came to visit, bringing with him a shit tonne of delicious wine.

The winemaker was Eulogio Pomares and he is the maker of some pretty killer drops in Galicia, Spain. Not only is the wine great, but he is also one of the leading figures in Galicia when it comes to sustainable viticulture. Unsurprisingly, he had some interesting things to say. The standout for me however, was his solution to the struggles of calcium deficiency.

Calcium is another mineral that the vines need a decent dose of to maintain their health. What is the normal solution? Spray and walk away, of course. But when this occurs, there is often an overload of calcium in the soil and this instability can cause damage to the ecosystem. So Eulogio found another solution.

He spoke a lot about the old ways of grape production and how there always used to be a solution, but nowadays we seem to have forgotten them, the sticking plaster approach of spraying crops being just too easy. Eulogio had heard of an ancient method, however: seashells.

Seaweed, like comfrey, has its uses in the vineyard, and for those by the coast this is not too rare. Seashells, however, are a little different.

"I just decided to ask the canneries," he said. "In Galicia, we produce a lot of tinned seafood, so I figured they must have a lot of shells left over."

Sure enough, he was right. He started to collect the shells, when needed, from the canneries to spread among his vines.

"It takes seven years for a shell to break down into the soil," he told of his discovery. "And as it does so, it releases the perfect amount of calcium to meet the vines' needs, while still keeping everything in balance."

I learnt a lot from Eulogio that day, but the greatest message that I took away with me was the one already mentioned, endemic within all of these practices: nature already has a solution. And we used to know it too. We simply forgot. Now though, I'd say it's abundantly clear (hello?! world's on fire!) that we have to jog our memories and go back to using them.

Mother nature will thank us, I am sure. And, in time, repay the favour.

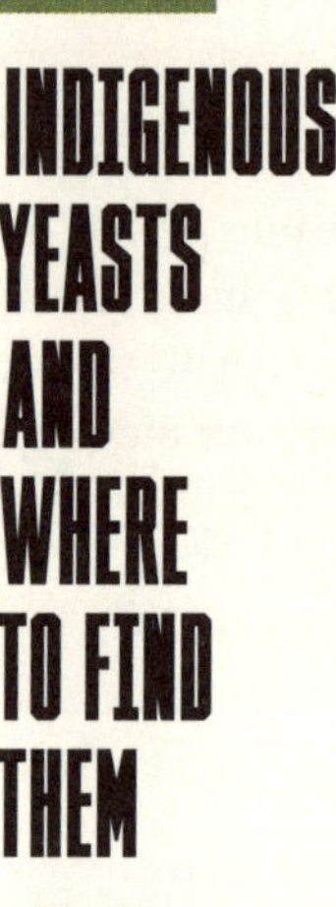

INDIGENOUS YEASTS AND WHERE TO FIND THEM

What a miraculous creature, yeast. It just brings us so many damn good things and it's so damn abundant too. Ready at a moment's notice to ferment any old sugars into something beautiful.

And it is because of this abundance that a lot of the world's winemakers want to be using the natural stuff, the real stuff, the stuff that is already out there, as a living part of the environment from which we take the very grapes we wish to ferment. It makes sense.

But for some reason it still is something of a radical thought. The big guys out there are still using the conventional lab-grown yeast. It comes in little packets, like for breadmaking. You activate it with some warm water, then you get it all worked up by adding some of the grape must. After an hour or so this shit is raring to go and you let it loose on the juice. Like a fox in a chicken hutch, it goes on a rampage and gobbles up every bit of sugar it can find while multiplying practically ad infinitum.

It does the job and it does it well, but there's a big trend back towards the natural ways of old. Using the yeasts that mother nature provides, the wine is likewise inoculated and the grapes go through their fermentation in much the same way that the store-bought fellas do. So, what is the difference, and why this debate?

Well, first let's look at Mr. Store Bought. Isolated from nature and bred in a lab, you get the perfect yeast. There are multiple strains of different kinds that all do different jobs. As in, for light red wines, use these guys; for bold whites, check out this model. The yeasts, like I said, are some of the same that occur naturally in the vineyards. But in this case they're isolated, meaning only the one you want is going to be present in the fermenting wine. These yeasts are consistent and thorough. They're specifically designed for the wine and they ferment and preserve the desired flavours.

These selected yeasts are also durable. There is such a thing as a stuck ferment, which is where the yeast has died off and stopped the fermentation, but there is still sugar within the wine, meaning there's also a lesser amount of alcohol than desired. This is often because the yeast, being sadly a suicidal fella, has killed itself off as it can't handle the amount of alcohol in which it is now swimming. This is especially a problem in hotter regions where the alcohol levels creep up a bit higher. Conventional yeasts can work well in this case as they will have been selected to withstand the higher alcohol levels. Sounds pretty good right?

But then there's the natural sort, and they can be rather interesting. The first thing to note is that wild yeasts are wild, meaning they are often a big mix of different types of yeasts that happened to be pulled on that day of harvest. This requires varying populations at different times throughout the ferment (different yeasts have different tolerances to alcohol, all taking their turn to leave their mark on the wine). In the process, these wild ones might be bringing in different flavours and characteristics, as the yeast can actually produce different esters (flavour chemicals) as well as the alcohol as it ferments. Tropical fruit flavours are an example of this. They occur anyway in the flavours of grapes but sometimes they'll be synthesised in the wine by the yeast. Most importantly these yeasts are true to the land. They're a little wild and unpredictable, yet they express the terroir honestly, providing a complete image of what is really out there.

That is where this more holistic view of wine stems from too. The more of the true environment that surrounds the producer and produce that goes into the wine, the more unique the product is. And in this way we can use wine as a spyglass to glimpse other corners of the world.

Natural yeasts are believed to deepen the complexity of the wine as they bring about those new flavours and continue to harmoniously mix them with the old. Although the big drawback to natural yeast can also be this same thing: unpredictability. This can occur in the flavour. Although it's rare, they don't always produce the most favourable of flavours, which can be a bit of a bummer if you're not into, say, the taste of banana in your red wine.

They can be slow too, and sometimes even incapable of completing the ferment, meaning that some conventional yeasts might be needed to finish the job. From what I hear though, this is rare, and the natural yeasts are able to work it through to the end. Still, these factors are often enough to dissuade the big producers from experimenting with it. They gotta watch their bottom lines, right?

It is an interesting thing to consider. My siding would always be on that of the natural, wild yeasts where possible. It's all about encouraging the holistic process and creating something that is a true chunk of nature, extracted from that environment and bottled up for me to enjoy. An honest thing that is truly unique.

When out and about, trippin' and sippin' and the like, I am often interested to hear of people's experiences with natural yeast. It can be challenging and it can be fickle. Sometimes it is the alcohol that poses the challenge and sometimes it is the temperature. A German producer I once met had the misfortune of a number of stuck ferments. He was producing wine up in the Mosël region of southwest Germany, in an underground cellar that was chilly on the warmest of days.

Yeast likes to be nice and toasty in order to do its job. If the temperature is lower, this tends to slow down its rate of production. If temperatures drop too low, as in somewhere near the freezing point, the yeast will stop altogether. This does not mean that it is done forever, as often it will continue its work as the temperatures rise again, excitedly popping back into action, shooting bungs across the winery or overflowing sealed and forgotten tanks (this does unfortunately open the door to other microbes, who will not perform quite as we'd like, so it can be a little risky doing things the natural way, as our German friend may tell you).

So, this Mosël producer mentioned that he had a wine that had been stuck in ferment for over three years. Every summer when the temperature would rise, a touch more of the sugar would slowly be consumed as the yeast would grind its way back into action. In that region, the summers are fleeting and temperatures would soon be heading back south, meaning the wine would go back into dormancy. By this point it had been three years and there was still residual sugar.

Man, I think about him often. Definitely every time I have the pleasure of drinking a German Riesling. I wonder if he ever got his wine. Or is the wine (and is he) forever trapped in limbo?

Thankfully not everyone has such difficulty. One clear and very warm day I was up in the steep-terraced hills of the Douro Valley. I had the extreme pleasure of visiting the proprietors of the Quinta da Costa do Pinhão, Miguel and Filipa (we heard from Miguel before, on the subject of pesticides). On that same trip, we'd had an excellent day surveying the property: a steep narrow stretch of land, carved into one of the valley's sheer banks which, starting at over 500 metres (1640 feet) above sea level, then plummets to around 150 metres (492 feet) along the Pinhão River, one of the tributaries of the Douro.

That day, the harvesters were hard at work on the terraces below the winery, picking that year's contribution of port grapes, which, due to their required extra-ripeness, come in a few weeks after the fruit used for the still wines. We had tasted our way extensively through the contents of each barrel in the cellar before sitting down to a long, wine-soaked lunch.

At a certain point the conversation switched to native yeasts. It was admittedly a niche crowd. These guys had inherited their cellar from the family, which had been constructed at some point early in the previous century. The old stones were full of good wine stories, certainly, but also good yeasts.

“There have never been any commercial yeasts used in this winery,” Miguel stated with pride. “Always we have fermented using native yeasts, in the old, traditional way.”

This was strict policy on their property, it turned out.

“I have had a few winemakers over the years who have rented tank space from us and I always have to tell them that they can’t bring in any yeasts.”

I asked Miguel why that was.

“Well, the yeasts are not just in the wine, but in the atmosphere around the wine. The yeasts we ferment with are sourced from the grapes and the vineyard, but also the winery itself,” he continued. “You often see wineries, with their marketing, stating things like ‘fermented with native yeasts’ but then they have a whole range of other wines that they ferment with conventional yeasts. These yeasts are the same, so no, you can’t really call them ‘native yeasts.’”

A very difficult thing to measure, but it made sense to me. We then progressed to discussing the whole natural-yeast-not-finishing-ferments controversy, at which Filipa retorted, “It’s a myth!” with surprising ferocity, more than I was prepared to argue with on a full stomach. That settled that then. But moreover, they had had some wines with wickedly high alcohol levels and never had they seen even one fail to complete its ferment. Perhaps there were one or two that had to wait patiently over winter, but that ain’t no thing.

So there it is, folks. The verdict is in: natural yeast provides the goods! And if you disagree, take it up with Filipa.

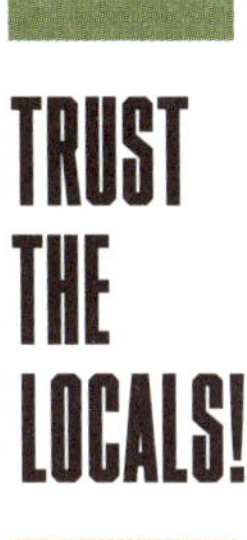

The wine world has become overly simplified. Nowadays, in a lot of places you can just bark some French sounding name like Merlot at the wait staff and they'll dutifully bring you something soft and red. Is it Merlot? Meh, who cares, right? It tastes more or less like it.

Now, I know this simplification makes it nice and easy for the average consumer. They haven't got to do any research beyond tasting maybe four different grapes and they can get the goods they're looking for. I guess this is no bad thing, right? Wait, actually no, it's fucking lame. This bullshit is what, up until very recently, was turning the wine industry into this big global factory spitting out identical copies of the same shiny new toy.

It still is in a lot of ways, but I feel like the engines are starting to slow. This model destroys the entire image of wine as this special thing that can only be grown in the right places, and when it is, it's something unique, unlike any other. A true gem. We've talked about terroir and all that jazz, so you know what I am on about. I guess this is where things get a little tricky. We want people en masse to have access to this amazing beverage, but we also want it to be something unique and special. It's a difficult spot with no right answer.

What I think is categorically not good though is the above model and what it has done to the world of wine, which is the widespread uprooting of native species to be replaced by one of the everyday varieties that everyone can pronounce, just about. These varieties are generally hardier than the natives, more resistant to drought, disease, and excess heat, for example, and they still put out quality wine, so they're a bonus for farmers too. More yield, less work. This is especially true in the New World system, which is the driver for a lot of these market forces. Out there, they chose only the best of the bunch with which to plant, influencing the entire rest of the wine growing planet, and it has come back to bite Europe in the ass.

As I mentioned, this does seem to be slowing somewhat now that there is a big (and growing) movement favouring native varieties in appreciation of the fact that they're unique. It is going to take a bit more of a push to get it over the line, but perhaps in a not-so-distant future people will be relaxed in the idea of drinking an unknown variety, simply selecting it from a description of its characteristics, which more often than not should be plenty to determine one's probable like or dislike of it.

But why is there a need to preserve these old varieties at all? There must be something deeper right?

Well, there is.

Despite the introduced varieties being hardier and more resistant to environmental challenges, there is the argument that they never really perform in quite the same way as the OGs. Take a Syrah vine in my home of NZ. Down in the Hawkes Bay region, among the alluvial Gimlett Gravels, this variety puts out some serious fucking belters. Now, the vines that are currently in New Zealand were most likely taken there in the last hundred years and now they are being cloned for planting far and wide.

For this is an important part of the theory too. Grapevines are never produced through natural reproduction, whereby an organism reacts to its environment and produces a genetic mutation that will—hopefully—possess some more adaptive traits and increase its chances of continued survival. The usual Darwinian stuff. Instead, a cutting of a parent plant is taken and stuck in the ground where it then grows some roots and goes from there. Growing vines from seed leaves too much to DNA's imagination and we're not taking any chances here. We want that same delicious shit that old mate down the road or back in the old country was drinking, so this is the way to do it.

Over millennia, this method will produce changes in the vines but not in the hundred-or-so year history of wine in NZ or wherever else in the New World. For the most part in these regions, the vines all across the country are genetic clones of the original plants that were taken to those distant shores, and they are only as equipped to deal with the local environment as the first parent plant was.

This vine is going to perform. Year after year, tough little fuckers that grapevines are, they're going to put out a lot of good grapes for the production of some delicious wine. The question is, however, are they really going to understand the terroir that they are growing in?

To put this in perspective, I have a friend who is a skilled grower of the devil's lettuce. This is all legal where he's doing it so cool your jets. We once had an interesting discussion about how he grows cannabis in a new spot. Seeing as, no matter the location, everything is farmed indoors and to the highest medical grade, one might simply assume that a weed grower would just stick the seeds in the soil and bobsyeruncle. That's not quite the case though.

He spent some time describing to me how he painstakingly grows the plant from the original seed, allowing this plant to produce its own seed, before rinsing and repeating. He must carry on in this way, producing numerous new generations, until he determines that the weed produced is up to standard and the plants are adequately adjusted to this new environment. Then, and only then, will he start cloning and begin the production process. And, like I said, this is all indoors, in a somewhat sterile and heavily controlled environment! Now imagine that out in the wild. Grapevines live for a long time and they are not so easily swapped around like weed plants in a hydroponics setup. It takes a long time for changes to take hold.

The alternatives are vines grown in Ol' Europe, like in some forgotten corner of Spain or Portugal. Most likely, these vines were carried here on the backs of Roman settlers in the beginning of the Common Era, if they weren't already there before thanks to the movements of even earlier people, like the Phoenicians.

The grape-growing folk would have gone about their business in much the same way, even all the way back when. They would have cut their clones and planted them where they had newly set up home base in their effort to get the wine flowing. I am sure they would have had a good basic knowledge about it too, knowing where to put the white grapes and where to put the reds. Or maybe they didn't. But by now at least, so much time has passed that the dynamic between nature and human acclimation has progressed enough to have corrected any initial flawed guesswork.

Regardless, over the following millennia the grapes were going to grow. Generation after generation then pulled up, cloned, and replanted the vineyards, and over time the grapes they were growing would have moulded to their environment and developed into entirely different varieties. Much in the way Darwin liked it, but in a more managed, supervised way.

Nowadays, the miracle of modern science makes it possible to look back through the DNA of grape varieties and see their ancestry. This has worked well in our favour, such as when scientists were able to figure out that Cabernet Sauvignon, much as the name may suggest, is in fact a baby made by Sauvignon Blanc and Cabernet Franc. This does not however work so simply for grape varieties that have been evolving in place for thousands of years. It is through this amazing process that by no coincidence Portugal seems to be rich in minerally, fresh white varieties, well adapted to coastal life, while the centre of Spain is full of robust red varieties that love the hot heat of continental living.

So now do you see the argument for native varieties?

They not only understand the terroir and all it gives and takes, but they are the terroir. I love getting into this subject as I tour the vines of Iberia, meeting with incredible minds of the vinous persuasion.

On one crisp early autumn morning, Amy and I were up in the Douro Valley and looking to get a little deeper under the skin of this famous region. People all around the world know what it is capable of producing, but I was confident there was more to the story than what the local wine regulators have quite bureaucratically mandated to be "wine of the Douro Valley." There's got to be more to the story. That day we had the extreme pleasure of meeting up with Luis Pedro Cândido da Silva, who is the loving and passionate proprietor of Quinta da Carolina.

Luis makes some incredible wines for the famous wine company Niepoort, where he is the head winemaker. This consumes a lot of his time but every spare second he has he willingly pours into his work at the Quinta da Carolina, a property his family has owned since 2004. You can see it holds all his heart and soul in the way he lovingly looks upon it and describes every inch of its detail. Despite his young age (which normally would mean limited experience, although not in this case), Luis is cheerfully confident with what he produces—and how he does it. Around things he is less sure of, he remains boldly ready to take the risk and learn. He has seen much of how things are in the Douro, as well as what is produced under these enforced styles of vineyard management. He has his own theories.

"And maybe I am not doing it right either. I guess we will see someday," he remarked with a laugh.

And what a property it is, where the mighty Douro River slides south around a bend, opening wide before it pitches westward again on its never-ending mission towards the coast, the banks rising high and steep. On the road that runs along this riverbank, an incredibly sharp hairpin turn, taken in a minimum of two attempts, brings the car round to a narrow, rocky driveway that climbs at an extreme angle and twists away among the trees. Pulling round a few more bends, you come to a stop at Luis's house, where he is already working away, barrels, buckets, and hoses in use, despite it being nine o'clock on a Saturday morning. Carefully tucked into the precipitous southern slope of the valley, just 100 metres (330 feet) or so above the smooth flowing water, the house (and winery) has a clear view of the precious vines that make all the magic.

The vines and vineyards with which Luis works are an incredible sight, too, of course. The sheer cliff climbs at a steep angle up from the river, to where the house is and continues up like a column for a few hundred metres more. About halfway up this bank, as indicated by Luis, is where his vines stop and those of his neighbour, one of the well-known local port houses, begins, which in turn climb to the top of the rise, towering high above us.

The vines beyond Luis's property are nice and neat, straight up and down and growing with a clear consistency. The leaves are thick on the vine and their colour is mostly consistent across the board, with only a slight change as the altitude increases. The higher up vines were already starting to hint at that autumn palette, but the change was gradual. Below this dividing line, however, the vines are very different. Each one has its own gnarly personality that grows and shapes itself according to its desire, all the better to enjoy its environment and capture the light.

Within the Douro there is a great advantage to ripping up the old and replanting. The yields are higher, the vineyards easier to care for, and you can choose the varieties that best suit your particular position in the valley. The usual stuff, right? This is especially true in *this* specific section of the valley, where the vineyards earn the highest grade, meaning a lot of clams are up for grabs. The bureaucratic local DO (Denomination of Origin) weighs in pretty heavily, unsurprisingly, but we'll get to that later.

Luis sees it another way. His vines were planted in the 1930s. They have seen a lot of tough years, from a variety of caretakers (of varying viticultural skills, too) over that intervening time. But each one is its own self.

"There are twenty-eight different varieties here that we have been able to distinguish so far," Luis beamed. "But perhaps there are even more, and even some that no longer grow anywhere else."

This added another dimension to my understanding of the vineyard as I gazed up again to take it in. Due to being all different varieties, each of the vines displayed leaves of different colours. Some had even dropped their leaves already for winter, while others were still green, only the edges showcasing the faintest glow of gold. All across the vineyard I could also see reds and oranges and yellows. A diverse array of sunset tones.

"I love the old vines and what they give to each year's wine. Each one is like a cocktail of different elements." Because the wines that Luis makes are always a field blend of what grows out there, each year it is different. "Some years it's lean like a yoga teacher and other years it is more robust," he carried on with a smirk.

This is due to differing conditions each year. In some years one grape variety or a cluster of them will prevail and influence the resulting wine's character; in other years another handful will do better than that rest, producing a different result.

The essential truth of the matter is that these vines, this wide assortment of different local varieties that have evolved there over thousands of years, reflect what the environment gives them. They don't always produce the same crop, as Luis will tell you; the quantities that he harvests each year varies greatly. They are, however, a true reflection of the terroir, unlike the sturdy vines of Syrah and Sauvignon Blanc, producing thick bunches of the same grapes year after year, taking on something of the terroir but not really communicating it as thoroughly.

That's why the local grapes should and hopefully will always prevail. They produce the best wine that the land can give. Wine that is of the Earth.

WITH THANKS TO THE EARTH

I mean, how could we not be thankful? The mere fact that we have the cognitive ability to be thankful is because the Earth is here, existing, allowing us to exist in the first place.

If you've ever had a moment to pause and reflect on just how remarkable it all is, you will know something of what I'm talking about. I hope though, that if you hadn't yet come to that realisation, the completion of this first part has inched that message closer to home. In a general sense, of course, but how remarkably this reverence for the amazing things our planet can do all fits together when we also consider how it helps us to produce our wine.

There are always a lot of competing factors at play within the wine industry, but if there is one message that I hope to impart from all of this, it is that we have got to keep protecting it. I, for one, am ceaselessly fascinated with all our planet gives and all it does and I sincerely hope that fascination never leaves me. I guess, in order to fuel the fire, I will just have to continue trippin' and sippin'. Twist my arm.

I know it's the message of the times, plastered everywhere from the biggest billboards to the smallest message about recycling that's printed on the labels of our food packaging.

But we can do this with our wine choices too. By drinking wine from artisanal, small producers who work in harmony with the land, we help ensure that what's in the bottle was produced by someone who loves their little patch of land and wants to see it continue to do its thing, in the healthiest way possible, forever, long after we've gone. They spend countless hours of their lives following through on this passion for the land and, thankfully, this shows in the quality of their wines too.

So, do your bit. Research the producers of your wines, find their message of commitment to the Earth among their marketing. If that's too much hassle, ask your local wine purveyor. I am sure they'll help. Small, local businesses are often the ones who will carry these special drops, so support them whenever you can!

Sometimes you just have to get stuck into that 3€ (£, $ or whatever) supermarket bottle, but when you can, spend a little more—it's often less than you think—to make sure you've got the goods in your glass. You'll love it, but maybe even more importantly, the world might last another day because of it!

And on that dramatic note, how about a little ditty?

THE STORY OF GOOD GRAPES

I once heard a little story.

Sit still and I'll tell you.

It is the story of good grapes.

So, we've all seen the grapes hanging on the vine,

Roots down deep, leaves in sunshine.

But the farmer soon noticed, the ways of the vine

Planted in rich soil, it grew leaves all the time.

The bunches of fruit, there were not many,

Were weak and watery, sugars not any.

So how might one stop this, the farmer pondered and thought.

Maybe if I cut the shoots, the vines' growth I'll thwart!

So this was attempted, and the farmer did see

The quality improve, better grapes on the tree.
But still not enough, the wine lacked a certain punch.
The flavour barely noticed as it accompanied the lunch.
So what could one try to better the brood?
Perhaps it was the dirt that soured the mood.
So vines were planted up on high,
Where the hilltop gleamed and shone in the light.
Here underfoot were rocks and pebbles
Instead of rich mud, once living, now settled.
And the water did flow, so the roots went deep
But less and less that vine did creep.
And in the winter, a yearly cut
Meant summer grapes were rich, what luck!
The farmer had figured, one little ruse,
Convince the vine of hardship, suffering, and abuse.
As a result, all of the vine's power
Will go to making babies that may prosper and flower.
And that is how we have the very best wine,
All from a little trick of the vine.

PART TWO

IN YOUR GLASS

It's a common saying among winemakers: you can't make good wine; you can only grow it.

This shows the importance of the land, of nature in what we drink. It is everything. As you've seen in the previous part, it governs all we produce and how we produce it (while also giving us the very tools we need for production). It is so magical, so beautiful, so incredible how the land provides and how it shapes the grapes to produce something unique to every patch of land there is. It's a source of profound wonderment that offers us never-ending opportunities for exploration, for resulting joy.

But there is of course a little more to wine. There's another side that is equally as fascinating—but for a separate bunch of reasons. This is the side that relates to the human hand. For millennia the grapes have grown and for millennia the human hand has collected them up, like a sculptor smooshing together wet clay to find form, and moulded a shape of their desire.

In this part, I hope you are pleased to hear, I'm going to delve into a little history. There are a lot of interesting myths and legends about the beverages we consume and I personally am enthused by every single one of them. I have done my research but at the end of the day, I'm here first and foremost to have fun and spin a few yarns. Just don't come crying to me if my answers make you fail your history test. That's show business, baby!

One interesting message that has been transmitted through all of this research and discovery, however, which is one of the things that I love most about wine, is that regardless of how much we advance technology, inserting more machines and extracting more money, the old, authentic, and natural ways of producing wine, the same ways in which it has been done since the dawn of civilisation, are those that always prove themselves best.

So, where to start on this next adventure, now taking place inside of the glass?

When the grapes first enter the winery is probably a good spot.

THE OPEN *LAGARES*

Fresh from the harvest, the grapes are ready, packed full of flavour. So how do we get the wine out? More specifically, where do we get it out?

The *lagar* is a great place. *Lagares* are not strictly unique to Portugal; I believe it to be another tool of the Romans that was slung far and wide across the empire, albeit one that seems primarily to have been kept in good use by the Portuguese. This tool in fact sets the scene somewhat for the Portuguese styles of red and of port, with their massive jammy fruit characters that are both soft and tight at the same time.

So, what is a *lagar*? Well, it's a massive shallow tank. Thank you for asking. Pretty similar in size to a kids' paddling pool. They are around 50 centimetres to one metre (20 to 40 inches) in height, usually with dimensions of about two by two metres (6.5 by 6.5 feet). Traditionally, these things are made from big slabs of granite and there are a lot of wineries that still have the same ancient *lagares*, now thousands of years old. Nowadays though, it is increasingly common to see massive shallow stainless-steel tanks doing the same job, bringing these classic tools into the modern era. When it comes time to harvest, the grapes are poured into these giant basins, and it's here that they undergo fermentation.

Why is this so special? Because this wide-open tank allows for the softest of macerations. Every time the grapes are handled or subjected to some process that assists the maceration there is risk of bruising the fruit, which causes their more acrid and intense flavours to be released. Thus, the more delicate the ferment and maceration, the softer and more rounded the fruit character is in the wine.

These *lagares* achieve this by providing a massive surface area for the grapes to come into contact with the juice. Every day during a red wine's ferment it is necessary to wet and mix the cap in order to improve the chances of a quality maceration. What is the cap? It is a massive pile of skins. During fermentation, there is a lot of gas being formed and this pushes the solids up until they are sitting on top of the juice. Left this way and you'd have a red wine that was more like a heavy rosé and you'd be pretty disappointed. Unless in the mood for a heavy rosé, of course.

To avoid this, you have to mix the skins back in with the juice so that it obtains that nice even maceration we're looking for. To do this you can use a pump, which sends the juice to the top where the trusty winery minion (me at an earlier stage) will then spray it evenly over the cap, eventually causing the skins to sink and mix in with the whole stew. There is, however, also a lot of red wine flying everywhere during this process. This is one method of mixing, but one that doesn't produce the most delicate result. It is efficient though.

A better way is to do it by hand with some sort of tool, in particular, one that looks like an oversized coffee plunger. This was another job of mine, performed dutifully at six in the morning most days throughout one harvest. I was working in New Zealand and every day as the sun rose I had to be out there, hand-mixing these six 20,000 litre (5300 gallon) tanks of the finest Otago Pinot Noir. It got me in good shape, that was for sure. There must be a fair dose of my sweat mixed in there, too. Be wary of any Otago Pinots from 2016, it could be the one. But yeah, this makes for some delicate maceration. The grapes are stirred back into contact with the juice and everything stays nice and tight throughout fermentation.

The *lagares* allow for a step above. Up until now, I have been talking about tall cylindrical tanks, as is the norm with wine fermenters. The *lagares* are horizontal, so already we have a lot of good maceration occurring on its own. This can easily be increased even more, you just gotta get your feet dirty.

Yes, that's right, this is where the foot treading comes in. The grapes are worked by foot a good few times up and down, sometimes with crews of people dancing through the *lagares* in formation, keeping time with some music. This process is repeated a few times throughout the fermentation to ensure maximum maceration. And not for nothing. The feet do have their benefits too. They bring around the softest maceration there is, as feet are soft compared to steel, while they don't rupture the seeds or skins too much, releasing unwanted flavours, and allow a good n' thorough mixing.

Sound gross? One thing to bear in mind when thinking about wine and hygiene—especially when feet are involved—is that this is a tank or vessel that is teeming with active microbial activity. Yes, it is necessary to wash your feet before you jump in, but any little nasties that do get in are gonna be killed by the other microbes as well as the alcohol.

In cases where feet are harder to come by (a day's foot treading can last for several hours and multiple days and require many participants), people use tools similar to the large coffee plunger I used. In some very advanced places, they even have robots that are set up with the plungers, all in a row, and the machine works back and forth over the *lagar*, just as foot-treaders would, but I suspect less jauntily.

The fact that people are looking for ways to mechanise the use of *lagares* and replicate the care that human feet are able to take shows that there must be some benefit to the wine made with this technique. Namely, this benefit shows in the taste. As I mentioned, *lagar* wines are usually very soft and round, much less likely to have any of the harsh tannins or green flavours which often come about when an extraction has been too harsh.

So, there it is; the first of many examples of why keeping it old school will always be the way. Of course, the *lagar* is just one of many vessels that can be used to make wine. Steel tanks, as I said before, are probably the most common in use today. There is also a lot of fermentation done in tanks and/or barrels made of wood. And a lot of wine is made in vessels made from clay, cement, and stone too. All soon to be divulged.

But first, what kinds of wines are we even making?

Just so that we're all on the same page, let's have a speedy look at the basics of all the wines we drink.

The first and most simple would be the white wine. This is generally made by taking grapes of the white variety and pressing them before any fermentation occurs. Usually, the liquid is squeezed out of the grape as soon as it enters the building. Bit of a rough introduction but it leaves us with some nice clean juice to then ferment into our white wine.

Then there are the rosés. This all goes down with the same process as above, however here a little spectrum starts up, with a lot of commotion resulting from just how much colour is put into the wine. First thing to know is that red grapes . . . have clear juice. (*Mind blown.*) OK, there *are* a couple with red juice, known as *teinturier* (French for "dry cleaner") grapes. A good example of this is Garnacha Tintorera or Alicante Bouschet, but most are not this way.

Some wines, those known as *blanc de noirs* (white from reds), are done with what is known as free run juice. This is where the grapes are loaded into a tank of some sort and the weight of gravity from the grapes pressing on each other causes juice to run out. This is most often clear at first and will make a white wine. Then, as further pressure is applied, some colour will start to be extracted from the skins. Sometimes this is done with gravity, other times with a mechanical press. The amount of pressure applied ultimately determines how dark the rosé will eventually be. There are even a few additional tricks involving steeping the skins in the juice—but you'll have to wait till the next chapter for that! As I mentioned though, the more colour that's pressed out of the skins, the darker the rosé, thus forming that spectrum from light to dark.

At the end of that spectrum? That's where our reds start. Red wines are made from the fermentation of the red grape juice in contact with the skins. When the grapes enter the winery, they are often popped and then all the mush is transported to a tank where it all ferments together. Just how much time each wine spends with its skins is what will determine the ultimate style and characteristics of the wine, but as you can imagine this allows for another spectrum from light to heavy and dark, with all this also dependent on the variety of the grapes and the amount of extraction.

There are a couple of other decisions affecting the red wine, such as the use of stems. Sometimes, you'll see that written on the label too. Something like "whole bunch ferment" or "fermented with x% of the stems." This trick relates to the more or less savoury character in wines. The berries themselves, as you probably figure, is where the fruitiness comes from, but the use of the stems can then bring it back the other way. The stems contain tannin too, as they're a little woody, so they can have a drying effect on the wine's flavour and thus a savoury influence.

So, that was the absolute essential basics.

How are we feeling? All set to continue?

Here is where things start to get a little more wild, so I hope you are pumped, informed, and ready to rumble.

Let us start with the question . . .

ARE THERE ORANGES IN YOUR WINE?

I've heard it asked a couple of times. It is something that really seems to confuse folks. If they're making it out of grapes, perhaps they're doing the same with oranges now too? Exactly *how* many oranges are in an orange wine?

Well, exactly none, naught. Zeeeerooooo! It's all just grapes, as it is with all wine. It's just a different process.

Orange wines are white wines that have been left to ferment in the same way that we make red wines. Remember, what we said about the reds. The juice soaks with the skins, right? And it is leaving the grape skins to soak in their juices that colours the wine and fills it with all the delicious flavours, aromas, and tannins. Now, if you do this same process with white grapes, the wine goes orange!

This is what is known in the white wine world as skin contact, and there is a broad spectrum for this, ranging from bright, lemony yellows to full blown marmalade-y brown. It all comes down to the time that the grapes are left to stew in their juices throughout the ferment. Like a tea bag, the longer you leave it, the stronger it gets. This can be anywhere from a few hours to a long, six-month soak.

A little side note: when talking about red wines it's better to discuss the degree of maceration that the red grapes underwent. All red wines have skin contact, otherwise they would be *blanc de noirs* or rosés. Don't be a banana.

But then grapes are more green than orange or yellow . . . So how is the colour created? It's pretty simple to see where the colour comes from with red grapes, but white ones? Not so much. A normal white wine grape ranges from vivid green to a burnt yellow. Certainly not this deep, orangey brown we see in the bottle. For this particular perplexity, I like to think of an apple. When you cut it open it's all green and fresh, but as time goes by and it sits there all sad and uneaten in your Tupperware, it starts to oxidise and the flesh's colour starts to stray towards an unappetizing brown. This here is the same deal.

It's a fascinating spectrum and the flavours produced are amazing. When making reds, the tannin is a big deal. This is pulled from the skins and sometimes, as we now know, from the addition of the grape stems if the winemaker has chosen to do so. As the skins are present with orange wine, the tannin shows up too, which makes for a rather different profile. The wines tend to be more textured than a normal white and they have the tingly, drying sensation of red wine tannins, although in a much lighter sense, similar to a cup of herbal tea. These tannins build in with a deeper complexity owing to extended skin contact, while lending the acidity a bit more tension, which can even extend to a sort of chewy sensation. The fruity notes are curious too, with apricot or herbaceous, geranium-like notes coming in at the lighter end, extending to wild marmalade or balsamic ginger notes at the other. Crazy stuff.

The concept of skin contact goes a bit deeper too when we broach the topic of cold soak macerations. I'm a sucker for a good bit of cold soak maceration, as much as the next man. This is the process of leaving the grapes to soak in the juice while everything is . . . you guessed it. Cold.

But how does this work?

So, white grapes (or red if making those heavier styles of rosé I mentioned) are brought into the winery and they are processed in whichever way the winemaker sees fit before heading into the tank. Here the temperature has been controlled with some sort of refrigeration set up. The grapes are thrown in and their temperatures are brought way down. So far down, in fact, that the little yeasties have trouble doing their job. This is usually around the 5 degree (41 F) mark. At this temperature, the ferment is suspended and the grapes can stew in their juices without alteration. Again like a teabag, more time, more goodness is pulled from the skins. This process is usually done for anything from a few hours to overnight, but in some cases it can last a few days. The grapes are then sent to the press, the juice is pumped back to the tank and things are left to warm up to a temperature that invites the yeast to get busy. From here, the ferment is pretty much the same as with any other white wine.

What's the point, you might ask?

Well, trapped inside the skins there is a whole host more flavour, aroma, and most importantly oil! And there's a good word I get to use here. Ready? Unctuous. When discussing a wine's oiliness we are discussing its unctuosity. Wines that have undergone cold soak maceration are a lot more unctuous, meaning they have an enhanced roundness, softness, or chewiness in the mouth. Just like comparing the texture of olive oil to water. The wines are denser too, with their flavour enhanced to a deeper complexity. The bigger body also gives time a bit more chunk to chisel so the wines tend to have a better ageability.

Glorious!

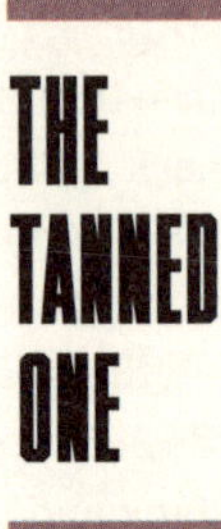

THE TANNED ONE

I have taken a fair few trips in my time and significantly more sips than that. So, as a person who never shies away from a glass full of near-on fuckin' anything, I've made my way through a decent few of the orange wines on offer in Portugal. The term used here for these wines is "*curtimenta*," roughly translatable as "tanned," but in this case relating to skin contact. All red wines are said to be *curtimentas*, but there are an increasing number of white grape *curtimentas* floating about, AKA orange wines.

This is no new concept to Portugal. White skin ferment, especially those brewed in *talhas* (the traditional clay amphora of the Alentejo region), have been carried out for donkeys' years, and there is definitely an edge to the selection coming out of these parts. When tasting orange wines from other countries, I notice their deep complex bodies and dark, rich colours. Here in Portugal, although some do achieve this sort of intensity, the wines are fresher: vibrant with racy acidity, bright with fruit flavours and tingly tannins.

The other big distinction here is the minerality. If there was one overarching word to describe the white wines of Portugal, this would be it. Mineral. If you've ever seen an atlas, you'll recall that Portugal is flanked by the

Atlantic Ocean and this wild and cold coastline it beats against has a powerful effect on the wines (I see you, DIURNAL SHIFT). But it goes deeper than this too. The grape varieties that have evolved along this coastline and deeper into the country draw from ancient stony soils and are swayed by stiff, salt breezes, the way they have since their time began. The resulting varieties found here are the very essence of this environment: fresh with sharp stony mineralities and cutthroat acidities.

And this extends into the *curtimentas*.

Instead of prolonged ferments and macerations, the *curtimentas* are usually only left to ferment with the skins for a brief period. Once the wine has reached its desired level of skin extraction it is pressed off the skins and from there treated as a normal wine. This period might only be a few days for the lighter ones. For slightly heavier wines, the skins can be left in for a bit longer, with the end of ferment (15 to 20 days) usually being the maximum. This shorter exposure to the skins, a few days or weeks instead of many months as they do in other places, means a limited extraction, which preserves more of this vitality and freshness.

André Lourenço is a pirate winemaker based in the Beira Baixa region near the town of Fundão. I refer to him as a pirate due to his experimentation with a large variety of different grapes that he works with a multitude of growers to produce. Not, as far as I'm aware, because he likes to plunder the booty of passing ships. André instead makes some wicked *curtimentas* and, interested in his methods, I asked him to weigh in on what he thinks makes them so special.

We sat down one scorching hot afternoon in Fundão to enjoy some lunch and a bottle of his latest concoction: an orange wine made in partnership with his father-in-law up in Lafões, a small subregion of Dão, just north of where he usually produces. The wine was tight and refreshing, but with just enough skin contact to have that bit of floral complexity, as well as a tingle of tannin.

"When you press and ferment white grapes, it's like you are leaving behind the grape's soul," he commented as we talked more about the concept of *curtimentas*. "There are so many precursors for aroma that are held within the skins. Most of that is tossed away when you don't ferment with the skins. After a while, keeping the skins with the fermenting juice, these precursors open up and the full aromas develop. The profile becomes whole, more complete."

Curtimentas seem to be popping up all around at this time, but maybe it's just something of a fashion.

"What does your father-in-law think of making *curtimentas*?" I asked him.

"Nothing really." Oh. A little anticlimactic. I pressed him to say more.

"He just sees them as white wines. This is how the wines always used to be. We were never in the habit of pressing the wine off its skins as we wanted the full expression of the grapes."

He recalled a time when, as a child, he used to go with his father to collect grapes from a local grower: "We would take them home and leave them all to ferment with the skins to make the wine for our family. This is the true Portuguese wine."

There is never a shortage of experiments brewing away in his little winery, which sits just outside Fundão, surrounded by cherry trees. After lunch, we tasted his most recent *curtimenta*, straight from the tank. The wine had a beautiful, bright golden hue to it, like the golden rays of dawn. Tasted like it too. Clean and sharp in the mouth but with a tropical afterglow before a soft tannin set in.

As André had claimed, the wines' souls did certainly seem intact, the nose so fragrant and zinging with acidity. It was a delightful thirst quencher that was much needed throughout the rest of that hot summer afternoon.

PRETTY AS A *PALHETE*

In the days of old, in the rural parts of Portugal, the general rule was if you wanted something you had to produce it yourself. Sure, there was plenty of bartering. Each neighbour would have their specialty and sometimes it was better to rely on the supreme cheesemaking skills of another than to produce your own. Wine, however, seems to have been a bit more ubiquitous. Every person who possessed a patch of land had the space to produce grapes—and the thirst for it. The vines would grow aplenty in any crack they could find, climbing up and around the house, their bunches hanging heavy in the late summer sun with sweet, sticky juice. Desperate for some fermentation.

This could easily be done in any household container, or alternatively by tossing the grapes into the neighbourhood pot to share the bounty out. Those with a little more space at their disposal could have more vines and would perhaps introduce a bit more organisation into the whole affair. The property's fences were near always teeming with grapes regardless of what went on in between. The owner might even have had a few vessels set up in their shed or garage. In Portuguese village life, wine is never far away. And in healthy quantities.

It may have been that the vines twisting through the property, planted long before its current occupants put down roots of their own, produced white grapes. Those would have most likely gone to making a *curtimenta*. If there were red grapes, perfect. Those would have made a nice red wine. But if, as often was the case, the grapes were a mix of different colours and not in a quantity to make enough of either option? Well, no problem. Just stick them all in together and get the yeast bubbling. This is what is known in Portugal as a *palhete*.

Within the communities of the countryside, where subsistence farming was often the way, this became a common style. As we discussed in the section on the *vinhas velhas*, the best results from the vineyard can often come from those in which the varieties are all mixed up, locking in that biosecurity. Where they have managed to survive, these vines can and do still put out an annual supply. And each year, following the land's providence, they give a different result.

A blend of both red and white grapes creates an even more varied palette from which to paint. The wines come out as dirty looking rosés. The shimmer around the edge comes from that white wine ribbon, but the colour is this gritty, dappled magenta. When done right, they are cutting with their acidity and almost smoky, with a plum jam sort of fruitiness. There might be ten different varieties blended together and they each seem to perform a vital part in the flavour, which is what makes this style so versatile and fun. In parts of Alentejo, namely Vidiguera, the fermentation process is often carried out in *talhas*, or traditional clay amphoras, adding yet another rustic dimension. With the soft ferment that these vessels allow, the wines are rounded, adding an almost chewy texture to the acidity.

My friends and I have passed many a scorching summer night at the restaurants of Évora with one of these delicious *palhetes* quenching our thirst. Ever exciting and a great match to a wide variety of food, they are just the thing for spicing up the mood. When it's hot out, *palhetes* can be served cold, the acidity and fresh fruity flavours taking over, the wine fresh and bright in the mouth. In the winter they can be drunk like red wines at room temperature, their smoky tannins mingling with the fruit to bring forth this warming intensity on the tongue. Whatever the weather, the *palhetes* will adapt. Just like the grape vines that make them, which each year adapt to what their environment provides.

These wines are as old as time, but I have a feeling we will be seeing a lot more from this style in the future. Once the word gets out, that is.

SOME LIKE 'EM YOUNG AND BUBBLY!

The wine world is always very occupied with age. And it's mostly concerned about the upper end of the spectrum. Oh boy, we want them as old as possible, blanketed in a thick layer of dust with a label that is barely legible.

Wait, do we?

These wines can be incredibly impressive when given the opportunity to taste them. But that's not all that wine is about. Wine is often an everyday experience and old bottles like that just ain't the way. There is in fact a midpoint where wines of quality have received the adequate amount of ageing to bring them into the peak performance zone. Yes, it is not only Usain Bolt who has one of those. Dependent on style and variety, wines need differing amounts of time to get to their sweet spot. Wines with big, robust bodies and harsh tannins especially need a good year or so in barrel and then even more time on the other side, in bottle, to really smooth out into something we want to drink.

I've had it from clients I have served before. That bullshit, "Oh god, these wines are just too young to be drinkable at all," as they turn their nose up at undeniably brilliant wine. These people have it in their heads that the only mark of quality in a wine is its age. They carry an annually moving mental note around with them: "Nothing newer than a 2017," they might say in 2023. Don't be that dickhead.

Here's why.

There is another end to the spectrum, where wines are made to drink as soon as possible after their production. The Vinho Verde in Portugal is one such spot. And it's a curious region, famous for its *vinho verde* or "young wine," but that's not how it got the name. In fact, at the conception of this region in 1903, it was more famous for the production of red wines than the ones they're famous for now. Located right next to the Douro, it often acted as a buffer for its neighbour. When the Douro was having a bad year and there was little wine available, the Vinho Verde region would step in to bolster the supply.

And apparently the name, Vinho Verde, came about due to just how green the land is. Pressed up against the Atlantic coast in the north of Portugal, this region is said to have more rain than the country of Wales. A country famous for its rolling green hills and . . . ? Rain. Lots of it.

In the 1940s things began to change. The region started to become known for this slightly green, fizzy white wine (they do the same process with red wines too, with some rather fun and interesting results). This is what the area is most known for now and it has even taken over the name of the region, synonymous with this type of wine ever since.

So, what is it really?

Well, this style of wine was developed in the countryside as something good and refreshing to sip away on a hot day, preferably with a plate of fried fish in front of you. They remain very traditional to the locals and many see it as *the* local way to make wine. Ricardo Garrido, our friend from the incredible Campos Masseira, fondly recalls how his grandfather would fill each bottle with his own homemade wine, adding a little spoon of sugar to each bottle just before it was capped—the perfect recipe for some fresh, zingy bubbles.

On the larger, more common scale there is an interesting and rather simple process used to produce them too. I like to call them "wines of impatience" as it seems that that is how they come about. The grapes are harvested, sometimes before they are completely ripe too, retaining that high acidity and that little kick of green grassiness. A simple wine is made with the pressed-off juice and when it is almost done fermenting that wine is bottled up. It is kept in storage for just a few weeks or months before it is considered ready to be consumed. And it comes out slightly green, with a big sharp acidity, a touch of residual sugar, and just a lick of effervescence where some of that sugar has continued to ferment in the bottle. These wines are delicious in the right setting. Just the thing for a hot day.

What about when it's a little chilly, though? Or really hot and the white just isn't calling you. In this scenario, I for one can say that I have on many occasions enjoyed a good drop of *joven*. This is the Spanish word for young and if you've ever sipped a few Spanish wines you may have seen this word thrown about. Unsurprisingly, it refers to young wines, but more so than that it refers to a style of production which has them tasting as good as possible as early as possible.

When making big-bodied reds, the aim of the game is a heavy extraction. Heaps of mincing and mashing of the grapes, seeds, and stems to pull out lots of flavour and tannin. That can then be moulded into the shape we want. For the *jovenes* there is a different aim, however. It's the complete opposite. You gotta treat those little grape babies so delicately that they only release their softest and most juicy flavours.

Here comes another term that you have probably got wind of before, and that is carbonic and/or semi-carbonic maceration. The most famous among these kinds of wines are the *en primeur* Gamays from Beaujolais. *Jovenes* are not universally produced with this method, like those Beaujolais seem to be, but the style definitely comes into play—at least the semi-carbonic—so I'll share a little taste of what goes down.

Carbonic maceration is all about carbon. Holy shit! Didn't see that one coming did ya? Alright, it's more about carbon dioxide but, y'know (*insert something about show business, baby*). For carbonic maceration, what they do is load the grapes into the tank, oh so very gently so as not to pop them, and then seal the tank up and pump it full of CO_2. The semi- way is similar, only they don't pump in the CO_2, instead allowing for whatever is formed organically from the fermentation build-up in the tank. The aim of the game here is to limit the wine's exposure to the grape skins and seeds—and usually, as these wines are often made whole bunch, the stems. When making a red wine, we are doing the opposite, in order to get more colour and tannin, but in the case of carbonic wine we want less of this.

So, the bunches of grapes are loaded very carefully into the tank and, by and large, they hold their structure—gravity of course squishes some at the bottom, but for the most part they stay whole. What then happens, which is kind of cool, is the juice actually ferments inside the berry, so now you have grapes with wine inside of them. The wine is then pressed out of the skins, again, gently, and you're left with this liquid that is all juicy, bubble-gummy, jammy goodness. This wine is gonna be rather light in colour, low in tannin, and high in delicate fruitiness as it has had minimal exposure to the mashed-up skins. After a bit of settling and a short rest in the bottle it's good to go. Although I know that there are indeed some producers in Spain doing the full carbonic maceration thing, I'd say most of what goes down is semi-carbonic. It occurs somewhat on its own when the grapes are loaded whole bunch and uncrushed into the tanks. Regardless of the exact way the *jovenes* are produced in each individual case, these here are the basics.

It makes for some fun drinking, especially when the weather is hot. These wines are awesome with a little chill on them. It's definitely the vibe in the wine bars of Madrid, which I have frequented on many a scorching hot night. The bar will have a massive, sweating bucket on it that is filled with icy water. Inside will be the bottles. Red, white, it's all the same—all served with a nice chill. That's when the *jovenes* are at peak, their juicy perfume popping like candy in your mouth. It's gorgeous!

So, in response to that silly statement, "the best are always the oldest," have you tried any of these youthful varieties yet? If not, go get yourself a bottle (and a leg to stand on).

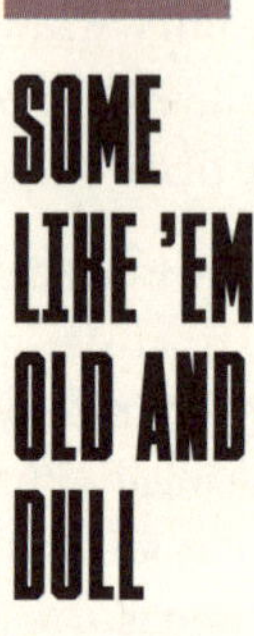

SOME LIKE 'EM OLD AND DULL

OK, age is not always so damn important as some might think. But there must be something to it. Some magic behind the madness. What exactly goes into all this ageing stuff then, that has so many people frothing at the mouth?

Starting out with our grapes, which we're going to assume here are of the highest quality, we generally have a few different roads we can go down. As detailed in the last chapter, we can make something easygoing and lighter by doing a gentle maceration, or we can do something a little more intense and then set it in barrel—or rather some other ageing vessel, such as clay, cement, even plastic. The big factor here is porosity (we need the bugger to breathe), so steel isn't going to be of use. By this logic, the plastic barrel may have you scratching your head, but worry not, they have developed these tanks from relatively porous plastic. Anyway, it's the time spent in the ageing vessel of choice that will be what eventually sculpts it into the shape we want.

The wine, be it red or white, is going to go into the barrel with a bit of punch. A heavier maceration—or in the case of whites, the deployment of more weighty grape varieties that have been grown somewhere that conditions are excellent (DIURNAL SHIFT!!!)—is going to produce a wine that is thick like syrup and packed full of fruit, acid, alcohol, and tannin. A sip of this stuff will send the palate cartwheeling as it tries to comprehend the aggressive explosion of flavours assaulting it.

Let's imagine that this wine, fresh off the press, is like a giant block of marble. The beautiful sculpture sits waiting within, but without a hammer and chisel, little will be revealed. Now the wine is pumped into its new wooden (or otherwise) home and time applies its slow, yet ever-helping hand. The wine will start to take on the oxygen coming through the porous vessel's walls. Simultaneously, whatever microbes are kicking about in there will spring into action. Slowly but surely, the wine, like the slab of marble with all its rough edges and lack of form, starts to be chiselled.

(The buzz words here are balance and integration.)

The first and most notable of the wine's changes—the first shapes to emerge from the marble—will be in the fruit character. It'll go into the barrel tasting like a fresh berry compote, straight out of the garden. It will be lively and young. Over time in the barrel, this is going to become duller, smoother. Just like fruit does when it is dried, the wine is going to start to resemble the richer flavours of raisins and prunes. In the case of some wines, this is going to change even more, with the fruit becoming savoury, giving hints of leather, tobacco, and even a full balsamic quality, balsamic vinegar just being super old ass wine. The ageing of this fruit is going to see it take up less room in the overall profile of the wine, allowing other aspects to come forward and creating that satisfying balance on the palate.

Another big player in the overall character of old wines is the tannin. Tannin is an odd little molecule which likes to suck things dry. It's what gives wine that astringent, drying sensation. Like the fruit, tannin starts out life loud and proud, boasting a lot to say. Over time though, these tannins will become less pronounced and are going to smooth out, to the point of landing with a pleasant tickle in the back of the cheeks instead of leaving you with oral discomfort akin to eating cinnamon. The tannin will also integrate into the overall body of the wine, finding its place of perfect harmony. What's really happening under the microscope is that the tannin chains, of which there are many, are binding together with the oxygen. This reduces the overall amount of tannin chains in the wine, which in turn starts to lose that bitterness and astringency. Leave it long enough, as is the case with some of those really old bottles, and the tannin chains will combine with each other to such a length that they'll actually drop out of solution and sink down as solid sediment!

Alcohol is an odd one. As we all know, wine is alcoholic. We like that. Alcohol can stay. It's the sensation of alcohol on the palate that is the problem here. In fact, one's ability to detect the alcohol in a wine can be a clear indicator of its true quality and, therefore, its value. Basically, if you're noticing the alcohol, you're drinking shit wine. We want that alcoholic smell and taste to be completely hidden, allowing the flavour to flow, smooth and easy. The sensory attack that one experiences when opening a bottle of nail polish remover is most definitely not something that should be experienced in wine. Thankfully, this presence of alcohol is another aspect that is going to relax over time. The grapes weren't always alcoholic; at one point not so long ago, they were just sugar. Now though, there's this new chemical sitting in the liquid and the rest of the liquid hasn't quite figured out what to do with it yet. But slap it in a barrel and time will see it take on a softer, more comfortable shape.

Here is where we need that other buzz word: integration.

The part of the wine that shapes things up in the barrel, ends up doing all the work, is the acid. Acid is the boss here. The one cracking the whip and making sure everyone else falls into line. The thing with acid is that it doesn't alter with time (OK, technically it does lessen over long periods but the taster's perception of it does not tend to change). It stays strong for a long while at least and it's the ultimate arbiter of the wine's balance. It keeps everything sharp, crisp, and working together as time evens it all out. Its presence is ultimately what stops all these competing elements punching each other to mush, so we must be thankful that it is able to endure.

Of course, it is difficult to discuss all of these aspects separately. They are having their effect simultaneously, in the same liquid, and it is their relationship to each other that brings about the overall change. It is incredible to note how they work together and bring about this transformation.

Before we get too far down the line, I should probably mention that not all of this is going to occur in the barrels or other large format ageing vessels. Such vessels are very porous and allow for these changes to occur at a rapid pace—if left for too long however, there is risk of overdoing it.

That is why we should give a shout out to the humble cork. The wine will be in barrel for a period of time, usually no more than 36 months, at which point, regardless of its state, it's better to put it into a bottle and let the ageing continue, yet in a slower fashion. The bottle is where the corks are the real hero. They have a purpose, you know.

Corks are made from the bark of a special type of oak tree, *Quercus suber*, that is native to the Mediterranean area. Portugal is the top producer, putting out around 70 percent of the global supply. All of this is grown within about three hour's drive from where I live, in the hot centre of Alentejo. The cork is particularly useful as it is able to be compressed without losing its shape or structural integrity. When it is squished into a bottle top it holds its form, sealing the bottle but still allowing air to pass through into the wine. It's this air, which the pro's call micro-oxygenation, that is going to produce the desired changes in the wine once it leaves the barrel. The cork allows the transformation to happen at a much slower rate and with a much more delicate hand. That's why it is common to see an amount of time stated for the period that the wine spent resting in the bottle on its tech sheets, as this often means that this method of development was important to the wine's evolution.

Today, we have a few alternative closures on offer, such as screw caps and even more novel containers, like cans. These are all great in the right context—which is wine that does not need any further ageing. Something like 80 percent of wine is consumed in the first two years after its production. Corks would have had little opportunity to work their magic within this timeframe and therefore it is somewhat wasteful to use them. Same goes for glass, which is heavier and less carbon efficient than, say, a bag-in-box or aluminium cans. The wine will be in perfect condition when it is ready to be served—but it won't ever improve. For wines that are worth the wait, those made to be aged and able to go the distance, cork and bottle will always be superior (again, the old ways can never be beaten).

So, while there is a lot that will change with the wine in the barrel, there is a likewise lot of change that takes place in the bottle, thanks to the cork. That last little bottle rest might make all the difference too, pulling all those developments together right at the end.

While all this is going on with the taste and flavour of the wine, there is also something else happening that's almost separate unto itself, and that is the colour. The visual imprint of time upon wine, its colour, is just doing its thing apart from the other elements. And this part certainly has its quirks too, with colour manifesting differently depending on the wine. Be it a white wine, the colour is going to start out as something light with that sparkling quality glass has. It catches the light. Time will see that colour darken as the wine concentrates. It'll drift from that shimmering sort of green towards a golden yellow, like a wheatfield at sunset (ahh).

Red is on another plain altogether. Like the white wines, they start out life with that bright sort of twinkling quality, but young reds are very dark. They have an almost obsidian-like depth to them and throw out some gorgeous shades of crimson and purple. In the case of aged wine though, time will see that colour lighten. The hue will fade and soften and the wine will eventually start to have a translucent quality to it.

What's curious about the two, is that their end results are something of the same. Both the red and the white wines will eventually decay in their colour to a dull brown tone. This doesn't mean that the wine will now taste bad, in fact it can often be the contrary, but it does mean that it is getting rather long in the tooth and that the drinker probably stepped in with the corkscrew at just the right time.

Old can be very interesting, and very delicious too. But young or old or in between, there are too many amazing things out there to be tasted. Therefore, the quest must continue!

Next stop is into the vessels themselves, which we use to make our wine. Because they've got some bangin' stories hidden inside of them too. The obvious are perhaps oak barrels, but we'll get to them. Let's start at the wild (and yet more traditional) end and work our way back.

ROMAN ROOTS

There are so many different subjects wrapped up within wine, as we've seen. It's not just a drink but a science, an art, a culture. A bottle captures so many great fields of knowledge, which constantly leave me in wonderment. Possibly the foremost of these would be the history. Everywhere we look today in this modern world we see gadgets and gizmos that, with each IOS update, take us further from our roots; from what we were before and, in a lot of ways, what we really need. I am no Luddite, but I do love any glimpse I can get into other times that came before us. And with wine, I feel there are so many of these little glimpses being frequently revealed.

Winemaking has been around on this planet for circa 8000 years. And alcohol production? Who knows. When was the first time someone's dear old mum forgot about the fruit she had picked and left in the old gourd round the back of the hut? They would have had a good party that night. Followed by the world's inaugural hangover breakfast.

It's been around forever though, right? And largely unchanged. We invest millions into the latest technology but the process never alters and never gets any better. Perfect as is, just like most things with nature. So many of the little tricks and techniques we use to procure this divine liquor have not changed since forever ago because it ain't broke. The phenomenon of living history is everywhere in the wine world, although one in particular stands out.

Big clay pots.

From a viewpoint in the city of Évora, where I have lately called home, Amy and I have often looked out to the horizon, across the lands of this part of southern Portugal, and daydreamed of the day when there were once Roman legions gathering there to move in and annex this land. For this area, the Alentejo, was what is known as the breadbasket of the Roman empire. Large-scale production of wheat was carried out here during those times that reshaped the culture and altered the land, forming the manmade savannahs that we find here today. Along with the bread though, the Romans needed to slake their thirst and take the edge off after a day's conquering.

Supposedly, due to the Phoenicean influence that came before, the Romans found the region already planted with grapes and producing wine, much to their delight I am sure, and would no doubt have quickly taken up the reins of production themselves. They did, however, add their own little touch, bringing with them additional techniques that would leave a long-lasting mark on the region. A mark that is still here today in the shape of the 2-metre- (7-foot-) tall terracotta *talhas* that are used with great love and tradition throughout the region.

These massive amphorae are, as sworn by many, the best way to ferment the wine. And they have gone unchanged for millennia (if it ain't broke, right?). But what makes them so good?

Of course, the big word here is "porous." This is the most important thing: these fuckers breathe.

When fermenting and ageing wine it is good to have a bit of oxygen in the mix. Just a bit though. As you know, the oxygen seeps in and softens those tannins; rounds out those edges. Dries the fruit and integrates everything into one fluid concept (pun intended). And clay, of course, has the same effect, being so porous. As the wine ferments, the terracotta is breathing and smoothing out the ferment (actually, double the amount of oxygen is able to pass through the terracotta as compared to wood, so the impact of the amphora is notable). This is particularly useful in the Alentejo region, famous for its soaring summer temperatures. Red grapes here can get pretty bold and aggressive, so this added dose of air helps to soften their punch. The extra air and porous breathability also helps to keep the temperature down. When the yeastie boys get going the temperatures start to rise and without a bit of control they can get so high that the fruit actually cooks. Well, it at least tastes that way; like a baked fruit pie. I can't fucking stand it. And I love pie.

Sorry natty wine kids, but natural is only cool if it tastes good. And this is especially the case for reds. The skins trap a lot of heat as the wine ferments. Then in the glass, the fruit gets all flabby, the alcohol jumps forward, and the acidity takes a hike. And all it would take is a little temperature control . . . Rant over.

But there are some natural options for resolving this and clay pots can go a long way. The breathability throughout a ferment means the heat is able to dissipate and the temperatures stay lower. The fruit character therefore has a good chance of staying fresh and defined. Not only that, but the lower temperatures actually slow down the ferment. We remember this from high school biology, don't we? That's why food goes in the fridge, where microbial activity is lowered. In wine terms though, cooler temperatures mean a slower, longer fermentation.

In other vessels, like steel, the ferment can heat up and finish much earlier than in the *talhas*. Nice guys finish second. The *talhas* facilitate a smooth and even fermentation as terracotta is not as insulating. This slowed fermentation helps to lock freshness and brightness into the wines as well, with the clay drawing out more acidity from the grapes as it reacts with the natural enzymes.

These *talhas* also have a way of naturally fining and filtering the wine. Getting all the gunk out basically. The free particles that come off the clay float around in the wine and bind up with the grape particles. Something to do with them being positively charged and the grapey proteins being negative. And, in a process that I like to call Magnetic Love, they attract each other and down they go. This all happens without the need for nasty chemicals that hail from dark places, like casein from milk, egg whites, or isinglass which comes from fish bladders (*wretches*) (side note, for those wondering: this here is often what stops your wine from being vegan).

Speaking of chemicals (this one is not that nasty, stop your whinging!), fermentation in clay also brings about greater phenolic extraction (phenolics = the green, leafy flavours), which aids in the stabilisation of the wine without the need for more SO_2 (sulphur dioxide). Pretty nifty, huh? And that's all before you taste them! The wines from *talhas* are always very rustic. Lots of grainy dusty tannin and aged fruit character. They taste historic, for sure. Even if made last week. There is a lot of funky variability among them too.

"It's as if each *talha* has her own personality that she gives to the wine," says Jorge Rodrigues of Outeiros Altos, a wine producer who ferments a lot of wine in 100+-year-old *talhas* near to the town of Estremoz.

The *talha* has been around the Alentejo for a while, but due to the rigorous, perfect-or-poison-yourself-trying winemaking trends of the 20th century they lost their popularity on the commercial stage. There was even something of a smear campaign against them, which pushed them further into obscurity. New measures around "hygiene in food production" that came in with help from the EU—starting from the 1970s, 'til maybe 15 years ago—deemed them as dirty. It was decided that clay pots (perhaps because they are made from dirt?) were unhygienic vessels for wine production and that they should be replaced with sterilisable steel. Thankfully, this didn't stick.

As tradition would have it, *talhas* remained safely in the care of the household winemaker, who had stored them in the gloomy depths of their tractor shed. The family's annual supply would be fermented in these, with grapes that were collected from the property or that of their neighbour. Piled in there, they were left to do their thing for a few months until the time came to hammer a tap into the base and pass round the glasses, always with a decent bit of fanfare.

Luckily, the wine world is open to more variability these days and winemakers across the region are putting in the effort to bring them back into common use. Not just as a unique way to make wine, but as something that is unmistakably Alentejo!

FORGING THE SEAL

Every now and then, when trippin' and sippin' through the wine world, one gets to witness something truly special. Something that totally warps the mind and reminds you just how deep and magical this topic is. Such an occasion occurred for me early one summer, not too long ago now.

Living in Alentejo, I had been learning lots about their traditional *talhas* and all the brilliant things they do. I had been doing a fair bit of research glass-in-hand-style too, if you know what I mean. Needless to say, they're well worth investigating. But there are lots of ways, less obvious than just the wine they produce, that make these vessels so interesting. I had heard talk of this process, what they refer to as a *pesgagem*, which involves sealing the clay to keep the wine in. Of course, I was very curious but, as I had also heard, these things don't come around all too often.

One morning, however, I happened to be mindlessly scrolling, as is the popular pastime these days, and I saw a post from a local winery, Gerações da Talha. *"Pesgagem das talhas amanhã,"* it said: "sealing of the *talhas* tomorrow." Instantly my mind started whirring. *Do I have time? How do I get there? Can it be done?* Needless to say, strings were pulled and I made my way towards Vila de Frades, a small village next to the town of Vidigueira, a well-known wine producing area in the Alentejo region. I had come to hear of this village a few times, a real hub for the *talha* producers apparently, so I was keen to check it out.

Before I was even in the right street, I could smell the smoke. Smoky smoke, it was, but with an interesting green note to it. I rounded the corner and the barrage of smoke nearly blocked my view. Up ahead, the massive *talha* was standing, upended, with the flames rising up around it. I rolled up to the scene, where I was warmly welcomed by Teresa and João, who run the show, as well as the amassing group of local oldies that had come out of the woodwork to inspect whether things were going as they should.

Inside the winery, there was another group too, working on another *talha*, curiously rocking back and forth. I came to learn that the project was started by Teresa's great grandfather. It was he who built the winery and installed the *talhas*—*talhas* that were already old when he got them!

So these massive clay amphora were over 250 years old, with some being even older, and all this time they had sat in this small village churning out wine year after year to keep the locals stocked up. One of the guys working on the *talhas* jokingly said, "They don't start to make good wine until they're over 300." Or maybe it wasn't a joke. They would know though.

As well as the wine production over all these years, there also had to be some maintenance. And as you would expect, this too is all done in ancient fashion. The task at hand was the *pesgagem*, which I mentioned is the process of sealing up the clay. As we know, clay is super porous, allowing lots of air to move through it. This means however, that without a little TLC they can also leak wine, which is bad for business if you intend to then try to sell that wine. So it must be kept within the vessel. To do this, a special resin has to be applied to the inside of the *talha* to form a protective coat. I was told that this is only necessary every 15 to 30 years, so it's kind of like Halley's Comet for the wine world, making me very lucky to witness it.

As both João and Teresa are young; they haven't had to do this too many times before, so the wisdom of the old master was necessary. Marcelino Pereira had come in early that morning from deep in the Alentejo region to show them how it was done. For 48 years he had been making wine and always in *talhas*: "Always have, always will," he assured me.

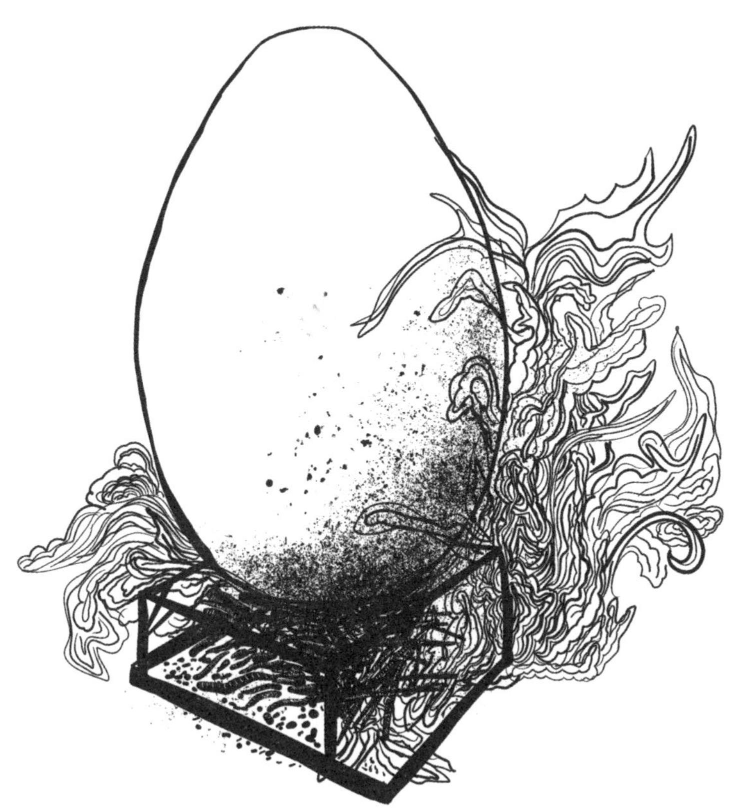

I asked him why the *talhas* are so special.

"We do it because it is the traditional way. And it is the best way. The wines have so much character." As he spoke, he was bent over the fire that was blazing up the side of one of the *talhas*, mixing up a mysterious pot of dark frothing liquid that boiled in the embers. This contained the fresh batch of resin that would coat the inner walls of the *talha* and keep any wine from leaking through the clay.

"You have to mix two parts of pine resin to one part beeswax," he instructed sagely as he stirred, the same instructions that had no doubt been handed down, through many generations, to him too.

Meanwhile, the flames continued their assault upon the *talha*, out of which smoke had begun billowing from its drainage hole, now sat upended at the top. Once it was too hot to touch (and they had all made sure of it, touching it with bare hands that were quickly snatched away again), the time came to lift the great vessel—with the help of a tractor—onto a pallet, ready to be shuffled back into the winery. Whilst the others did this, Marcelino carried his small cooking pot, still bubbling, into the building, where he then tipped its contents into the hissing clay amphora.

The roof hung low within the cave-like, 200-year-old winery, which was full of *talhas*. The room was also soon filled with sweet smoke and, as everybody coughed and spluttered, they began the sealing. They have to heat it up first to melt out the old resin, but also to make sure the new resin meets a surface of an equivalent temperature, allowing it to slowly coat the interior and not dry up too quickly. Once the resin was inside, I watched (or glimpsed through squinted eyes) as one fella, standing at the mouth, started to paint the interior with a makeshift, moplike brush, while the others slowly rotated the vessel, allowing him to get at all the sides.

Everyone lent a hand, either holding the *talha* in place or rolling it back and forth as the smoke rose and they coughed and joked. The young ones yelled at the older ones to get them out of the way, while the old ones yelled at the young ones, telling them what to do. So, all in typical fashion. It seemed at one point that the inside had been sufficiently coated and the fella with the brush took his leave, coughing, heading off to soothe his lungs with a cigarette outside. Now the inner wall was coated. But there remained the issue of excess resin still stuck in there.

Next, the group appeared whose job it was to rock the large amphora back and forth and side to side. "We're rocking the baby," one laughed.

Slowly but surely, the excess resin dried out, leaving an even coat around the whole interior. A last bit was painted onto the base and around the drainage hole to keep it all sanitary, then it was ready to go. All hands were once again on deck as the *talha* was lifted back upright and they shuffled it through the winery to its resting position. Finally, after they had it where they wanted it, they wedged it into place with some blocks of wood. The process complete. Just in time, the beers were passed round.

The next one was just getting hot on the fire outside.

There's a lot of wine out there that's all about the wood. The use of barrels seems almost synonymous with wine, don't ya think? They have been around a heck of a long time too. For thousands of years, people have been using some form of wooden vessel to store as well as age a variety of beverages.

They're handy when moving wine around as they have a solid shape and are not as fragile as materials like clay, used to make the beautiful *talhas*. In fact, wood has been pretty damn popular for the storage of wine throughout the history of trade. And today, they are easily the most common vessel to use in the ageing process.

But why is it that we like them so much? Is it just their durability during transportation?

As I have learned, when it comes to wine, there is always a little more to it than that. The big thing about wooden barrels, similar to the clay, is that they are porous. This means a healthy dose of oxygen can work its way through the wood and into the wine. Given a bit of time, that oxygen will play a large role in shaping up the final drop. We know that not all wines are barrel-aged. The springy, sharp white wines and the bouncy, juicy reds never see the inside of a barrel, while the smooth, robust monsters do. And it is precisely due to the use (or not) of barrels that we have those varying ends of the spectrum.

Much of the ageing of really old wines, like we discussed in the previous chapter, is done in the bottle, with the cork allowing oxygen to pass through. The thing with the wooden barrels, however, is that they've got a much larger surface area that the wine will be exposed to. This means the ageing and shaping of the wine happen at a much faster pace. In fact, you can select your barrel size for precisely this metric. This isn't unique to barrels; it is the same for all porous vessels.

So, what is unique to wood?

Well . . . it's woody. The barrels are highly prized for giving that woody character to the wine—another trait so common to wine that it could be mistaken for being ubiquitous. This character is such a mainstay in our wine experience, especially in the reds, that it might even surprise some to know it isn't naturally occurring. For those wondering, these are what are called the "secondary aromas" or characteristics of a wine. The primary being those given by the fruit, whilst the tertiary elements are those that develop in the wine as it ages in bottle, the secondary aromas are those that the wine has taken on during the winemaking process, which includes the fermentation and the barrel ageing.

If wood is the chosen vessel, a variety of different woods can be used, from acacia to chestnut, but of course oak is the classic choice. American oak is good, giving more intense notes of roasted coffee or tobacco, but most people will tell you that the French ones are the best in the biz. It is widely believed that the more subtle notes of vanilla, nuts, and honey are better for the wine, so the American ones are generally pushed out for winemaking, reserved instead for the bourbon, unless we are talking about the wines of Jerez.

The world of barrels is seeing some evolution these days—beyond just these two. The French have been struggling to meet demand and people are finding that oak from places in Europe are capable of similar things. This has meant that it's now somewhat common to see barrels of Romanian or Hungarian origin dutifully ageing the wines in cellars across Iberia, with the results coming out the same (or imperceptibly so, to my happily ignorant palate). Whatever the origin however, each of these different woods will leave their own impression on the wine, which will then integrate with the other flavours to define the final drop.

The other important thing about the barrels is their age. It's common, particularly in the case of white wine, to see terms like "25% new oak" or something similar on the label. This percentage tells you the quantity of new barrels that were employed in the ageing of that vintage. For example, 20 barrels were used in the making of that year's Tempranillo. That would mean that five of them were brand new barrels fresh from the cooper (the guy who makes barrels). This figure doesn't say anything about the barrels' porosity, as all are by and large the same (changing somewhat depending on the different woods); it speaks really only to how woody the wine will be after being aged in the vessel. New barrels, filled for the first time, have a lot of woody flavour trapped in them that is dying to be released into whatever liquid used to fill them. As the years pass by, the new barrels will eventually lose their super woodiness as more wine is exposed to them. The winemaker might then have this little factoid scribbled on the label to keep you in the loop.

"But what is the big deal about all this BS?" You might ask.

The wine world, for those brave enough to have lifted the lid a crack, is considerably wrapped up in all this BS—about how much French oak and how new it all is and so on. All of which really relates to another much deeper topic, or two in fact, that underlie this fixation.

The first is what I have come to refer to as . . .

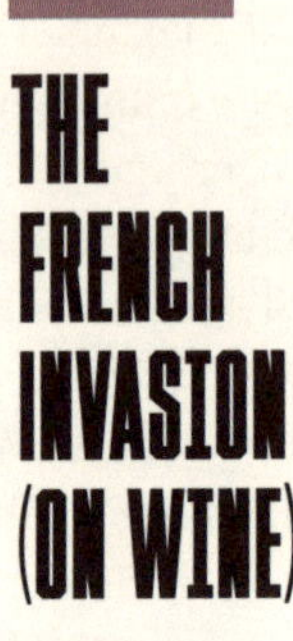

OK, it sounds a little intense. Sorry Frenchies, I don't mean to say that you've barged in here and fucked it all up. I have nothing against a good drop of French wine—I just don't have the same love affair with it that I do for the Iberian kind. But that's neither here nor there. Well, alright. Quite a lot of it is here.

Look, before you lose your head, let me explain!

The French invasion on wine is this concept that I have heard little inklings of in a few different places. There are whispers of it in the most forgotten regions, where it is a wonder that time reaches at all. In other regions it seems to be the theme that is blaring from a horn in the town square, as if mandated by royal decree. Because this is something that is now woven into the fabric of how these regions produce wine.

To get the gist of what I am referring to, we need to go back a bit. Back to when the world was suffering under the plight of that notorious little mite we know as Phylloxera.

As discussed in the previous section, the whole damn place was a shitshow then. A few lucky regions were holding out and providing wine for the parched masses still circling around the old, now dry, watering (wine-ing?) holes but most were in total ruin and had to be started again from scratch. Luckily, the grafting solution came to the rescue and life was once more returning to the wine world, but things would never be quite the same.

Prior to the influx of that bastard mite, the scene was very different. All across much of Europe—and especially in Iberia—the old style of planting was still prevalent. This is that *vinhas velhas* stuff we talked about. All the vines mixed together and planted in any random order, not necessarily in the neat rows we know today and not just grapes either, but with the odd olive, pomegranate, or fig tree thrown in the middle. The wines would follow suit too. A big old field blend would be sloshed together in any number of differing vessels from clay, to wood and even glass. Basically, blissful anarchy. The world was free to make the wine how they wanted, how the local tradition foretold, or however they could.

But then Phylloxera came and bare earth replaced even the most prized vineyards.

Over the next few decades a lot more came with the turn of the century, which included the invention of the tractor and the perishing of nearly all of the continent's men in the awful wars that devastated the first half of the 20th century. In the wine world this was obviously a time of great change, and it was at that point, over the course of the century separating the arrival of Phylloxera and the end of the Second World War, that heads turned to the French.

They had initially caused this whole Phylloxera thing, or at least the outbreak had originated in France after French viticulturists brought the American vines back to Europe, and they were at the forefront of solving the issue too.

This was also at a time when, much like today, the French held the world's attention when it came to quality wine. The best in the world were and still are purported to be of French origin, so something was being done right. The French grip on the quality wine market had taken hold throughout the Middle Ages, thanks to Britain's thirst for it. As the main consumer market for wine, the British had, for centuries, been drinking Western Europe dry. Then there were the wars.

Which wars? Well, too many to count from the 1100s to the 1800s. Between the 16th and 18th centuries was when things got especially tough for French wine in Britain, however. Excluding some trade with each country's respective colonies, British demand made up the majority of the foreign export market in those days. All these ongoing, little wars, as well as the new supplies of other delicious shit from places like Portugal, for example, therefore put the Brits in the driving seat, and their king drastically raised the tariffs on French wine. Not all French wine, just the bottom of the barrel crap. The bulk stuff. Of course the king still wanted a healthy supply off the top shelf (*wink wink*). And it was this little tax window through which the French would slip. They started to overhaul their wine industry in hopes of attaining the finest quality, leading to a lot of investment and reinvestment and a general "all boats rise with the incoming tide" sort of approach. The French wine industry committed itself to only producing the best, and this has a lot to do with why it still dominates (should we let them have it, or give all the credit to British high standards?).

After all this had gone down and out the other side, the "French way" had become the gospel on how to make good wine. And the gospel goes as such:

- The vines should all be planted in neat rows, to allow the tractor or horse (or whatever tool was necessary to aid in the work of the vineyard in the absence of all the workers—as later became the case during the World Wars of the 20th century) to move easily through the vineyard, thus speeding up the work.
- The best wines are to be made with a single variety, not this sloppy field blend muck. Extra points are awarded too if the variety is well known to consumers of French wine. So, kiss goodbye to your beloved ancient cultivars, for now the vineyards need straight rows of Pinot Noir, Syrah, Cabernet Sauvignon, Sav Blanc, and Chardonnay. They are good hardy varieties that will adapt to most new environments (maybe except for Pinot Noir) and still put out a good, clean crop. And most of all, they will sell!

- In the case of blended wines, these are OK, but they should be of no more than say, three varieties and the blend should be made after the wines have been distilled—again, none of this field blend shit, where the diverse array of varieties are all fermented together. *Non!* The wines need to be made first and the perfect balance must be struck between the competing varieties so as to make the best wine.
- Wines should be fermented and stored (when not in oak) in steel or concrete tanks. This is the clean way to produce wine and any other vessels, such as Alentejo's beautiful *talhas*, are dirty and disease-ridden and will only produce inferior wine.
- Oh, and last, but not least, everything, except the zingier white varieties, should spend a little time with some oak so that it can learn some manners and behave as we see fit. And to be exact this oak should be *French*, none of that heavy-handed, caramelised American stuff.

Of the Iberian countries, Spain would have to be the one who changed most in the face of this new style of production. Phylloxera had left their vineyards, which covered vast swathes of the country, bare, creating a huge pressure as well as incentive to conform. The country had always been an enormous producer of wine, as well as a heavyweight exporter, so they had to be up on these new industry standards. Plus, they wanted to maintain and improve the quality of their output and this was apparently the solution.

For the most part (and thankfully, I'll say), Spanish natives stayed in the dominant position, but at the same time there was widespread introduction of those "better," now highly common grape varieties. There are still many old plots of vines and a wide array of gorgeous indigenous varieties that are making their mark on the global market, but the number of regions with unique native varieties in Spain seems to be a lot less than over the border in Portugal. There are a few champions that have risen above the rest, such as (and not limited to) Tempranillo, the Cava grapes and Palomino Fino in Jerez but, with the exception of sherry, French style is usually employed to both grow and vinify the grapes. I don't mean to say this is a bad thing, merely an observation. Although, I can't help but wonder what was lost when all these changes from foreign soils came into play.

Portugal, on the other hand, has always been somewhat content continuing at its own pace. It marches to the beat of its own drum. There are multiple reasons for this.

One being the port industry. These guys won in this arena early on and that solidified the continued presence of the main port grapes in the country. Another would be their relative insignificance on the local scene (no offence Portugal, love you!). This small nation, stuck way out on the western edge of Europe, is dwarfed by the three biggest giants of the wine world, Spain, France, and Italy. Beyond these three, there are so many more countries producing wine that little old Portugal has just been left to its own devices. This has meant low prices for amazing quality wine, which is perhaps what has led it being the highest consumer of wine in the world: each person in Portugal consumes 51.9 litres (13.7 gallons) of wine a year (2020). It is also for this reason that today there are still 250 indigenous varieties commonly used in the country. I'm sure a couple of these are double-ups due to each region having a different name for each grape, but still, it's a lot. Now don't get me wrong, there has been a lot of Frenchification here too with many of these "international" (AKA French) varieties moving in, but a lot is done with the old cultivars too. There are some stunning super old vineyards here that really show that stark difference to the modern way.

And it is somewhat lucky for the Portuguese too. While doing their own thing all these years the tides have now started to turn in their favour. The French grip on the wine market has weakened considerably as the world enters a new era. Bordeaux has become something of a has-been and now people look to these outlying countries to provide them with the next new and exciting hit. New oak, with its smothering, overwhelming effect, is out, with winemakers now preferring the influence of neutral, well-used barrels, also entertaining a whole host of different vessels, both ancient and traditional, as well as modern, to store and age their wine.

Most brilliantly of all, it is the age of the indigenous variety—there's nothing quite so unique to a place as what has evolved in those very soils and now the world is thirsty for it. Portugal sits in a good position. There is so much that is truly unique going down here: the sky's the limit. Spain is in no bad position either. There may be a few wounds to lick but for the most part there is still a lot of beauty in the indigenous varieties the country possesses, regardless of how many were lost. I just hope that in the future we see a lot more of the rare ones popping up to add further texture and nuance to the country's already stunning offerings.

To sum up, during the 20th century, we witnessed the French invasion on wine. Did they teach the world the best way to make wine, or just white-wash everything, painting over all the unique identities? Perhaps the New World needed it; they needed some direction. But here in old Europe, is that necessarily so?

What I'm saying is that the commercialisation of the wine market, the globalisation if you will, was led by France's example in sending their wine to the far reaches of the globe. The rules were clear: field blends should make way for mono-varietals, and those grape varieties should be only the ones that sell. No more ancient varieties—tear them out!—and in their stead we want Syrahs and Chardonnays and Pinots and Sauvignons—be it Cabs, Francs, or Blancs! And the world listened. The New World sees few varieties other than these mighty soldiers, tried and true. But in the Old World, a lot was lost. A lot of heritage and beautiful biodiversity that would yield some superb flavours. Thankfully, this is not the reality across the board: pockets of resistance remain. Pockets which are now making a bold comeback, as trends bend back in their favour.

We can't blame it all on the French. Shit went down, they did their bit and wine continued on, mites be damned. There was one other big influencer though. One that has hit these shores a lot more recently.

So we had the French persuading us all to produce in their style. But they weren't the only ones making an argument for a homogenous market. Perhaps we should lay a little blame on California too.

The Californication of wine seems to have had a large impact on the produce of Iberia as well as beyond over the last few decades. Unlike with the French invasion, we don't have to go back so far to trace its origins. There was a big movement in the New World in the 1990s (or thereabouts), starting in particular, as you might have guessed, in California—and even more particularly in places like Napa.

These guys were growing some punchy varieties, like Zinfandel and Cabernet Sauvignon, and they figured out that aforementioned trick with the oak and how it manages to smooth everything out. Going a little bit further, they also figured that grapes of lower quality could be upgraded with a heavy maceration and a lot of oak ageing. Sort of like ironing out the wrinkles on a dress shirt, they could make wines of a consistent quality, regardless of what the vineyards were doing. Not just this, but these New World drinkers, who were just starting to get into their wine in the grand scheme of things, found that they quite liked their big oaky wines. Or at least this is what they were told by their fearless leaders, the heavy-handed wine reviewers of the time. You may know the gang to whom I refer.

So, California got into it and became the home of the oaky behemoth wines we now know them for. There was one little hiccough though, and that is price. Because California, as the fifth largest economy on the planet (yes that's right, California's economy is bigger than that of most countries), has always faced a real challenge in getting the price down. Land in this here state is very expensive—and that is obviously just the beginning. From there, the costs only mount. As the old saying goes, if you want to make a million bucks making wine, you have to start with four. This is certainly the case in California (and the USA in general) meaning their domestic wine was never cheap. And to top it all off, America was thirsty, goddamnit! So, they started to look around the world and, specific to this story, back over to Europe.

The reviewers pulled out their pens (I imagine them like big bingo markers, although this is probably not the case) and they started awarding high ratings to those that fit within their special standards: big and oaky. The population followed suit and guzzled down these "90+ pointers" with gusto. The reviewers continued and even started to point out their favourite regions. The Priorat, La Rioja, Ribera del Duero, the Douro, Alentejo. They all and have always produced some pretty powerful reds—what would happen if we upped the oak? Said regions responded by stamping these styles into their rules and the money flowed towards those that were able to produce in this style. The wines were good and everyone enjoyed them. But the wines seemed to lose their honesty, their own character, what made them unique.

It is rather difficult, as you might imagine, to taste the subtleties of an indigenous grape or a prized patch of land when it's drowning under the weight of mammoth amounts of oak. It's an interesting time we're living through: in a lot of ways this Californian influence has done Iberia a lot of good, turning the drinker's attention to what people are doing out here, but it is good to see winemakers of these same regions now drifting apart to produce wines that really reflect the land and the all varietal characteristics on offer.

Of course, the money from this demand was also useful. It raised the standards of production across the board: winemakers far and wide across Iberia have been able to hone their craft to a sharp point and have access to all the requisite fancy equipment to put them on the map, as well as having, most importantly, higher hygiene standards (I mean high cleaning standards in the winery were more easily attained as a result of this cash flow, not that ol' mate finally started to shower). Now though, the course has been primed and it is exciting to see the shimmering plethora of different wines being produced.

There has always been a lot more freedom in the more obscure regions. Where regulations are less tight (and not geared towards these market influences) winemakers produce more of whatever it is they fancy. In the more famous regions, like those mentioned above, it is fascinating to notice the difference.

On one trip through the stunning valley of La Rioja, I was lucky enough to meet with Carlos Mazo. Carlos is a dazzling producer within these famous lands who is newly on the scene, producing some spectacular wines.

He had taken us to see his vineyards that evening. It was late autumn to early winter and the sun was very low in the sky by the time we had driven the winding dirt track out the north side of town, Aldeanueva del Ebro, to his patch. Not only was it dusk, but a thick blanket of fog had unfurled across the land. The moisture hung thick in the air and we could scarcely see more than a few metres in front of us. The fog was so thick, in fact, that we nearly managed to sneak up on a pack of wild *javali* (boar) who shot off through the brush as Carlos's truck pulled up at the edge of the vines.

It was a beautiful vineyard, the vines all in goblet style, their thick arms sticking out in four directions, their roots in the soft clay and loam soils. They had been planted there by his grandfather and, unlike the usual Tempranillo which, owing to a few of the reasons mentioned above, have spread like wildfire across not just the region, but the whole country and beyond. These were a mix of varieties like Graciano, Garnacha, and Mazuelo. I was curious to know what it was like to produce wine in such a classic region, how might one distinguish oneself. His answer was rather fascinating.

"One has to make the wine and then work to understand what comes out," he started. "Then one has to strive to understand where it came from, the vines themselves and the varieties that they are. *Then*, it is important to assess what truly makes them unique—big bodies and high alcohol levels can be found anywhere," he continued. "The true beauty of one's particular region is found in that thing which sets them apart, which refreshes the senses."

He finished by saying, "Once one has found this, the task is then to extract it and bring it centre stage, but it is important that the higher in quality the wine is, the finer and more elegant it should be to really express that unique difference."

This is the philosophy that Carlos uses to make his wines and they really do shine with a different light to the rest. True to his word, as we progressed through a tasting, eventually arriving at the ones he sources from select, special vineyards, the winemaking became more precise, the wines lighter in style. What started out as a bold, deep purple-red colour progressed to a more translucent shimmering crimson.

Philosophies like this are changing the game when it comes to seeking out the finest of wines. And as the wine world begins to recover from this Californian hangover, we are left with more space to marvel at what these already stunning regions may come to signify in the future.

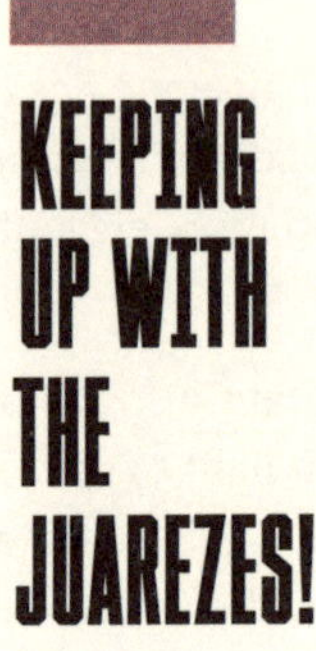

We talked all about the wild and incredibly unique island that is Lanzarote in part one. What an amazing place. The ravaging winds, the loose *picon* soils, and the wonderful little divots they dig to shelter the vines. There really is no place like it. It is amazing terroir and it sets the scene for some incredibly unique wine. And it is for that reason I was left with the inevitable question: where the fuck is all this incredible juice? All we could find was this over-oaked crap.

As I mentioned a few chapters back, I had done my homework and reached out to a short list of special producers who seemed to be doing things differently. You know the way we like it: low intervention, clean, healthy farming and the like. But as I also mentioned, none of them ever got back to me. I was cut off from the cool stuff. This was on that same trip when Amy and I had been sippin' in some of the top spots of Tenerife, so I figured maybe we'd already used up all our luck. Not letting that or my flashbacks to playground exclusion deter us too much, we were happy enough to cruise around the island and try some wines from the bigger names on the scene.

We were staying in the most picturesque little town, which provided quite a sight for sore eyes (and egos, for one of us at least) as we headed out and over the hills. Picture stark white moulded buildings rising out of jet-black soil beset with black mountains and vivid blue seas. Continuing through this rolling landscape for a while, the vineyards soon began, with their tell-tale little divots, to spread across the view in front of us.

We spent the afternoon driving around, pulling into the large car parks of these surprisingly packed wineries to try their fare, one after the other. I think three in total. I am sad to say, what we found was rather terrible. The wines were thin and lacklustre. The reds stood with wide arches and nothing to support them. Like houses of cards, they toppled inwards as they moved across the palate and disappeared before they were even half-way down the tongue. The whites, marginally better, had something of an interesting fruit character but limp-dick acidities that meant they too, fell short of gracing the end of the palate.

Seriously. What the fuck was going on?

To be exact, in such a unique and distinct landscape, why were the wines not made to express this? This got me thinking about the Californication of the wine scene in Spain, which over the last few decades has come to define the Spanish wine scene—at least in the mainstream. The mainland is all about big reds. That's what gets the folks' attention. That's what sells. So where does that leave Lanzarote? Well, they must follow suit. Surely they too can produce powerful reds that stand bold with firm structure, bolstered by crispy tannin. Right? Well, no.

This is a little volcanic island, with a lot of wind and a maritime climate. Sure, they get a lot of sunshine hours, but the nature of the soils and the climate is predisposed to produce wines of keen acidity and fruity precision. The heavy macerations and powerful oak, a piece of cake for the robust bastards of the continental centre of Spain, don't work the same and leave you a wine that is hollow and flabby. A pale imitation of their idols. Because the desired structure cannot hold if there is nothing to support it, the whites are suffering something of the same too. Barrel ageing and overripe fruit is not going to fairly express what the land provides, which again should be tense acidities and mineral fruit characters.

It is not my intention to destroy the image of this island's wine scene. If anything, I hope that this kind of criticism can be taken as constructive, and implore them to make some changes, to do things in a way more suited to their unique environment. I also hope that the more artisanal producers are already doing this (although I can't testify as a witness), as I can tell you there is a lot of individuality to be showcased from this island.

Have you ever heard of Lee? Or perhaps better put, the lees. Well, the lees are some interesting lil guys. And if we're gonna talk so much about the barrels it's probably best we mention them. Rude not to. The wood and its porosity does a lot, but there are often other helping hands at work, all pushing towards the same goal: wonderful wine. The lees are one such helping hand. Let me introduce them to you.

The lees are basically all the solid crap at the bottom of the wine tank. When the grapes come into the winery they do their ferment, on or off the skins depending on the style desired. At some point, they are pressed off the skins and the wine is transported to a holding tank or barrel. It's around this point here that a thick muck starts to accumulate and sink to the tank's base, leaving the once cloudy wine clearer as the dust settles. In this case though, the dust has more the texture of wet pottery clay and it smells like wine that's been baked into a cake. It really clings to your hands too.

This sludge is made up of all the dead yeast cells that came into existence during the fermentation. From the starting culture, they multiply at the rate of knots and then ultimately die when the alcohol gets too high. These cells are all mixed into the wine during and after being pressed, giving it a cloudy, muddy puddle look, but when the wine is left to settle they all sink down to the bottom. Sounds kinda gross, huh (sorry, Lee). But it's some super useful stuff. The trick is, you want to leave the wine to hang around for a bit with these guys still present, let them enjoy some quality time together in your tank or barrel or whatever vessel you choose. After a while, it starts to build all sorts of character into the wine.

The first and foremost of these characters being a deeper, richer complexity. As the yeast starts to break down it releases all sorts of proteins into the wine that manifest as biscuity, nutty, or sometimes creamy notes on the palate. Not only this, but they also build in a load of texture, making the mouth feel smoother and more rounded. There's a lot more aroma as a result too, and it's those proteins at work. They interact with the wine, releasing some volatile compounds that, to us, can translate as tropical fruity notes. Of course, that same bready, bakery note comes out too.

In order to maximise the contact the wine has with the lees, a process called *bâttonage* is employed. This is where the winemaker will come along with a special tool that looks sort of like a hockey stick and insert it into the barrel or vessel to mix everything up. This process will be repeated at regular intervals as the wine ages. Over time, a lot of those proteins will dissolve into the wine, producing the desired result.

They'll often boast about it on the label too. Something like, "Aged on lees with weekly *bâttonages* for 24 months" to explain how they got to that complex, vinous result. Because it is this process that often separates the youthful, fresh, and green styles of wine, like those made from Savvy B, and the richer, full bodied, and stunningly complex wines, like the big bastards that are made with Chardonnay.

When making Champagne, a wine style known for its bready, yeasty quality, each bottle goes through a process called riddling, where it is periodically rotated by a slight degree. Every time it's moved the lees still present in the bottle are stirred up, exposing the wine to more of their influence. The bottles then go through a process called disgorgement, where the lees are removed from the wine before they hit the market (that's why the wines don't have any sediment in them, just FYI). A lot of the flavour that's built into aged Champagne is done with the help of the lees though, which is why it's got that biscuity, brioche thing going on. And it genuinely is the same flavour involved in breadmaking—hence the direct comparison.

Yeast is a fascinating thing and the number of different uses it has in the production of quality wines is truly a wonder. It can be the gift that keeps on giving long after the wine has been bottled too.

André Lourenço, that brilliant producer in Portugal's Beira Baixa region whom we met earlier, shared one of his lee-based hacks with me, which all his many wicked wines are subject to. He had just poured me a taster of that *curtimenta* I mentioned before. The one that was bright like the morning light—you remember from my poetic description, right? It was beautiful. The *curtimenta* too. Well, we were discussing its clarity and colour.

"That is not how I bottle it, though," he commented. "I like to stir up the lees so it's cloudy when it goes into the bottle."

So, cloudy as it goes in, but then once the wine is able to settle the lees will sink to the bottom of the bottle, creating these little dancing wisps that float up in the wine when it is disturbed.

"It means the wine gets another *bâttonage* every time the bottle is moved," he said, resulting in a wine that continues to build with a particular yeasty complexity long after it has been bottled.

He then took a sample from another tank, one he'd recently churned up, and we were able to taste the two versions of the same wine side by side. One clear and settled, the other foggy with the lees. It was a very interesting experience to see how they compared. The clean wine was sharp and lively with a clear and direct floral fruitiness; the other possessed the same characteristics, but the acidity was softer as it hit the sides of the mouth, while the yeastiness made the wine's soft tannins more perceptible.

Side by side comparisons are always fascinating, showing just how deep the variability in each drop of wine can be. This one with the lees was no different. There are so many little tricks and tools that can be employed to ensure high quality and diversity in the final elixir. Although lee-ageing is not the most important of these, it holds its rightful place among the ranks of do-gooders.

Keep an eye out for it: you may be surprised what treasures you unearth.

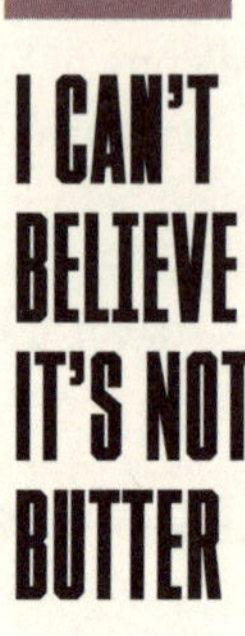

Like it or not, I'm sure you've cracked open a bottle of big butter Chard in your time. A lot of people love to hate on this style of wine. And there are a few producers out there who have perhaps leant into the gimmick a little too much. The competition as to who has the most butter in their wine may at this point have gone too far. Just a tad. Wouldn't you agree, California? The thing is though, it's another little trick in the winemaker's toolkit that can make for some incredible textures and complexities in wine, and I feel a little divulgence is in order.

So, butter, or more broadly stated, creaminess: what's the deal and how is it getting into our wine?

If you can't believe it's not butter that's probably because, in a way, it kind of is. Or similar, anyway. The cause of all this butteriness is in fact due to a curious process called malolactic fermentation, or malo for short. First, we have the alcoholic fermentation—that's the essential one. But then there is sometimes a second ferment that takes place. This mostly occurs in red wines, with basically all of them going through this process, but it can occur in some white wines when desired too. Most famously? In that big-butt Chard.

Malo is a secondary fermentation that generally comes about when a wine is left to rest in barrels. It can occur in tanks as well, but this usually only happens when the tank has been inoculated with the bacteria. In barrels, this fermentation usually occurs naturally. Also, we call it a fermentation but it's actually what is known as a decarboxylation. A new wine will have a load of little acid molecules floating about in it. And some of them will be what we call malic acid. Malic acid is a big acid boy with four carbons in its carbon chain. As a result, it's pretty sour. And then, floating around in the wine, we've got this little bacteria, *Oenococcus oeni*. He loves to eat malics and when he does he somehow nibbles off a little carbon atom, which is released as CO_2 gas (it's this part that deems this process a "decarboxylation"). He then proceeds to poop out an acid with only three carbons in its chain. This smaller acid is called lactic acid, and not only is it a lot less tart than the malic acid, which reduces that super sour taste, but it is also creamy and soft. Lactic acid is the same acid that occurs in milk and dairy, which is what makes that creamy too. It's fucking crazy, I know.

So that's the deal. The wines are creamy due to the malolactic fermentation. Now combine that creaminess with the oaky, toasted vanilla-like character that the barrels impart and we can get that smooth buttery softness that we know and love (well, some of us).

In red wines, this same fermentation is used to bring around a greater complexity of aroma and flavour, as well as a reduced and softer acidity. The reds that have experienced this process are noticeably less tart and they have soft, rounded edges. The creamy butteriness isn't so obvious but the textures are all there. The effect it has on white wine is the most distinguishable, however, and it produces some really cool wines. Obviously, it is most famous for use with the Chardonnay grape, but if you start to take note you will find that a lot of white wines which have seen the inside of a barrel have this same creamy quality and, like the reds, a deeper, more complex flavour and aroma profile. All thanks to this process!

Crazy little bastards, them lactic-acid-forming bacteria, right?

Ok, so we've gone over the basics. The usual stuff: how we ferment the grapes and how we usually go about ageing them into something drinkable.

Time (and a lot of patience) is one of the ultimate keys to good winemaking that should never be forgotten or overlooked. There are of course some prime examples of this being taken to the extreme. And as you might imagine, the results of this time and patience can be jaw-on-the-floor-holy-fucking-shit kind of interesting. This one is a can of worms, so I will warn you, it's gonna get deep and maybe a little weird. Hang on to your hats. This is quite possibly the most delicious can of worms you'll ever open, though, so it's got that going for it. That is if you like your worms nutty, musty, and sort of damp. Mmm.

If you know you know, but if you don't—I am talking about sherry. And no, the real stuff is not fucking sweet, but dry as bone! Nor is it just a drink for the grandmas of the world. It's actually good, OK? Just listen.

But just before we get into sherry we have to talk about *soleras*. *Solera* is a system of what's known as "fractional blending" that was developed in

Spain. They do it in other places and may have even done so for longer for all I know, but meh, Spain's where it is at. They go hard. And the majority of it is all concentrated around one place, the city of Jerez de la Frontera (pronounced "Hereth") which sits at the top of the very southern tip of Spain. With Jerez as the capital of this little winemaking region, the town of Sanlúcar de Barrameda should also be mentioned, as they are right next door and also deal in this wizardry.

Winemaking has been around these parts and northern Africa since the Phoenicians were here, some 3000 years ago. This style of winemaking developed in the last 500, however, but I think we can all agree that's a decent amount of time to be working on something.

What is this style then? Like I said, it is a system of fractional blending, which basically means mixing a small fraction of new wine with a larger fraction of older wine. This is done to give the effect of rapid ageing and it adds all sorts of interesting and very complex flavours and aromas. It's a fascinating process that started in an interesting way too. See, this region used to sell a lot to the British. This is probably sounding familiar by now.

(*Good Middle Ages rule of thumb, if you wanna be successful in the wine biz, stay friendly with the British. 'Cause, boy, did they guzzle it back.*)

However, the Spanish did not stay friendly with the British, of course. Things were very tense, in fact. Henry VIII had decided to bin off Catholicism, so he could in turn bin off his dead brother's wife who he had decided to marry for some strange reason. She, Catherine of Aragon, was Spanish, so there came a wee problem there. What really got the Spaniards' goat was the whole Catholicism stuff. Both the state and the Pope were, in effect, "a bit miffed."

This was also at a time when the Spanish, thanks to the Austro-Hungarian Hapsburgs, owned the Netherlands and there was a lot of shady plotting going down. Sir Francis Drake then smashed in the city of Cádiz in the 1570s and had come back to England fucking loaded with wine. The Brits then came to love a drop of their "Sack Sherry," a fortified sweet white wine, probably similar to today's Moscatels from Setúbal. So the Brits had a taste for it now. And they were fucking thirsty.

Tensions continued to mount. Then in 1588, when the Spanish had collected up all their ships to send them to the Netherlands ready to invade England, all hell broke loose. The English sank the majority of them in the English Channel. This was indeed the famed Spanish Armada; a battle that became a major part of what is known as the Anglo-Spanish wars. And what this meant was . . . no Spanish wine in England!

Suddenly, Jerez was awash with wine but with no buyer in sight. The barrel halls filled and still more had to be built, only to be filled again. The odd buyer would come by, such as some fella from France and old Klaus from Germany. They'd take what they could, but it wasn't enough to lower the supply. Upon purchase, the winemakers would syphon off the desired amount, topping up the barrels with other, newer wines to keep them from spoiling. Until they started to taste . . . a little funny. Very different actually. But really rather fucking good.

The wines were generally fortified; that was a given, something that had become commonplace since the introduction of distillation by the Moors, who also spent some time occupying those lands, so they were built to last. But time in barrel, and the frequent syphoning off and topping up, had produced a unique and continuously evolving effect: they kept getting better, nuttier, more caramel, even sweeter.

Then there were the wines that were unfortified, also building up in surplus and receiving the same syphon top-up treatment. When left open to the air, these wines would develop a thick crust over the top, similar to the exterior of old cheese. The flavours these wines would develop were also more complex, getting drier and nuttier with time. Through this far-reaching and incredible confluence of events and production techniques, the world of modern-day sherry started to develop. It began to weave itself into a fine, diverse tapestry, all in a little world of its own, which now leaves us with a fascinating range of unique wines.

This saw the development of the *solera*, named after the elaborate system behind this now time-tested and true process, which means to take from the ground or from the bottom. They do it by starting with their barrels stacked up. For simplicity's sake, let's say there are three barrels stacked on top of each other (there can be many more—five, nine, even fourteen!). The

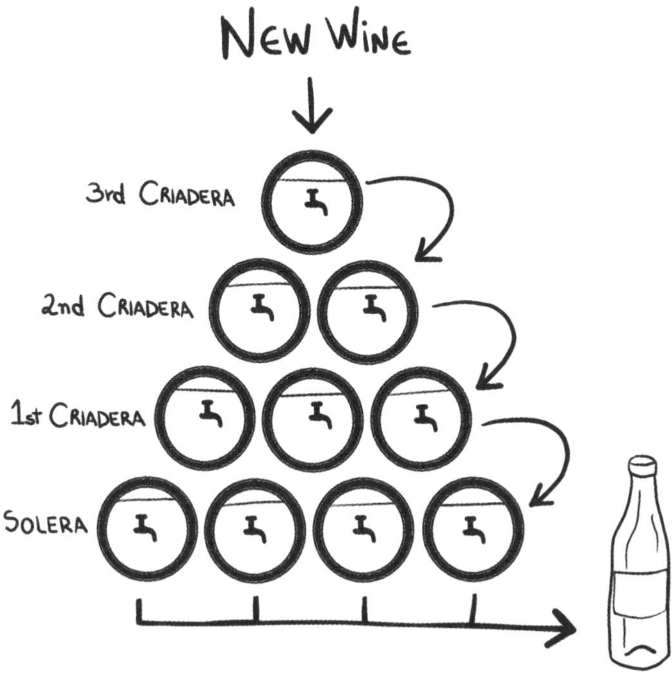

two barrels at the top would be what are known as *criaderas*, while at the bottom sits the *solera.*

Every couple of months, wine is moved through this system in fractions. It should be noted that the barrels are never full—only about 80 percent (more on this later). From the *solera*, roughly a third of the wine is taken out, and it's this that is used to fill the bottles which will be sold: the wine exiting this stacking system. But now there is a gap in the *solera* barrel. From the barrel above, the first *criadera*, one third is removed and syphoned down to fill the gap in the *solera*—and to fill the gap in this first *criadera*, one third is brought down from the second *criader*a, which is positioned at the top. The empty gap in the barrel has now been transferred to the top of the system. New wine is now brought in to fill this gap, and this is how the wine enters the system.

But it's the wine that remains in the barrels that's the real epic shit. This wine has been washed around in these barrels for, at the very least, decades. I have heard it said that a *solera* under 50 years old is practically useless for putting out sherries of decent *crianza* (the term for ageing). Most are well older than this. They've been going for generations, with the oldest continuous one going from 1789, currently owned by Bodegas Alvear in the Montilla Morales region, near Córdoba. One other way to put it came from a guide I once had around one of the gloomy old bodegas of Jerez: "I never met my grandfather," he said. "He died before I was born. I never met my great grandfather either, nor the people before, but the wines they made are still moving around in these barrels and I am connected to them as long as I continue to work here."

What this means, however, is that there is no way to start a new *solera* system; we can only continue those that are already in motion, which shows us something of their rarity and need for protection.

Now let's talk about scale. It can be quite comical really. As the scenario often goes, you are given a random address in the city of Jerez and upon arrival you find yourself in a long, seemingly dead street, lined by white-washed walls with no windows, punctuated only by the occasional minute door. Nowhere to go. But then one of the little doors creaks open, an old hand protrudes, and you are beckoned into the gloom. As the eye gets accustomed to the little light that pokes through the thatch in the rafters, you suddenly feel the expanse open up before you. The Big Bang in sherry terms. A warehouse the size of a football field is revealed, with barrels stacked high like the walls of a maze, and you are smacked with the musty odour of this miraculous elixir.

These barrel halls are enormous, with often hundreds of barrels forming each stage of the *crianza*, millions upon millions of litres in these 500 litre (130 gallon) casks of blackened, pungent American oak—yes, remember what I said before? American oak is not generally popular for winemaking, but it does have its rightful place in Jerez, where the sherry's caramel nuttiness is well complemented by the toasty intensity bestowed by this variety of wood.

I love to consider the word "spirit" when I think of sherry. We refer to liquors that have been distilled as spirits, right? But to make them, wine or another alcohol is put over a fire, the spirit boiled out with hot, brute force.

With sherry, it is just wine. But it is wine that has been flushed through this distillation system, the impurities and excesses have evaporated and what's left is the true, dancing spirit of the wine: a dazzling elixir.

Soleras are the tools developed to achieve this end. But what then are all the different styles? We're getting there. First, there is an important division between the two groups.

One group is fortified. This means a decent whack of *aguardiente* (the name for Spanish brandy, or "fire water") is added to the wine before it is left to rest for a long, long time in barrels. This whack of *aguardiente* stops all types of fermentation and allows the wine to oxidise—for however long is desired—without altering its state too much. In this way, the higher alcoholic content acts almost like a preservative, keeping the wine safe as it develops richer riches and complexer complexities.

The other group is a little more interesting. This is what is referred to as the natural sherry category, as the wines are left to age naturally, free of any fortification. How this occurs is with that crust I mentioned earlier. This is formed by a few beautiful yeastie boys all with the name *Saccharomyces*, which are collectively known in Spanish as the *flor* or flower. Remember, the barrels are never full—there is an air pocket at the top and it is here that the gang goes to work. They form what is known as a yeast cap: a musty crust (sorry) over the top of the wine. This yeast cap, known in Spanish as the *velo de flor*, is what mitigates the wine's exposure to oxygen, consumes any residual sugar, and concentrates the naturally forming glycerol, all providing a bit of that musty, bready sherry flavour. This is what makes the wines that are aged with *flor* lighter, drier, and livelier.

Now the actual styles that are written on the label.

It should be noted that all of these wines are made with virtually one grape variety, Palomino Fino, a fresh yet complex white grape that is abundant in this part of Andalucia. No shit. It is grown in this region of southern Spain in their incredible *albariza* soils, which are super chalky and sandy, stark white in colour. It makes for quite a sight. Chalky white soil, almost like snow, green vines and then the bold blue sky . . .

OK, no more daydreaming. The styles.

The first being Fino, the fine one. The youngest of the sherries and most comparable to white wine. This wine has passed through the *solera* system quite rapidly and has made many stops; sometimes up to nine barrels are used, with movements happening every few months for a total of around three to five years. This is a natural sherry, so unfortified, and it is aged with the use of the *flor*. These wines are super dry and chalky, with a lively sharp acidity and an opaque, greenish, straw-like colour.

This is also the same production used for the wines known as Manzanillas. These wines however, are not produced inland, in Jerez, and instead are produced some 30 kilometres (18.6 miles) away in Sanlúcar de Barrameda. This little town sits at the mouth of the Guadalquivir River in the gulf of Cádiz, soaking up that salty sea air. It is this that alters the wines. The ageing warehouses are found throughout the town, breathing it all in and putting out wines formed in the same style, from the same grape, but markedly different. They are more floral, saline, bitter, and damp, which is how they got the name Manzanilla, after the Spanish word for chamomile.

The next, and my favourite, is the Amontillado. This name means the wines are in the style of Montilla, a region near the city of Córdoba where it is believed this style of ageing sweet wines originated before Jerez stole the crown. Amontillados start their lives as Finos, passing rapidly through the barrels for a number of years until reaching a diversion. This diversion sees them put into yet another set of barrels where the movement slows down. At this stage, the *flor* starts to fade as there is little to sustain it, so the wine gets a little whack of *aguardiente* and then settles in for a long rest, moving between the barrels infrequently for up to ten years. With this one, you really see and taste the dancing spirit. The colour has started to turn to a dazzling golden-brown hue like a sepia sunset and the flavour has deepened to nutty complexity with notes of caramel and tobacco. The acid is still kicking, however, so the wines are persistent and fresh while still bone dry.

The next one is Oloroso, the pungent one. This fella knows only the fortified road. New wine is blended with *aguardiente* to raise it to around 17 percent—this is where the *flor* cannot form, usually tapping out at around 16 percent. And then it enters the *solera* system, where it can take up to 20 years, with infrequent movements, to go through to the bottle. These wines are also bone dry, as visible when looking at their glucose levels, but as they were not aged with the *flor* there is no consumption of glycerol, meaning over time this concentrates as the water evaporates and gives us a wine with the appearance of sweetness. When it comes to sherry flavours, these fellas are the whole hog too. They are dense and rounded with these fuller, balsamic depths alongside their deep nuttiness. They are as rich as rich gets and a single sip will have you inhaling and circulating within their aroma for a good few minutes after swallowing.

And then the wild card: Palo Cortado, "the cut stick." This one is rare and it's a fun one as it's got a little bit of a rebellious streak. Palo Cortados start life as Amontillados. They get up in the morning, they do the *solera* thing, they're home for dinner. But then something else starts to develop in the barrel. The winemakers will notice that there are some unique characteristics present. Characteristics that separate them from the other hundred-or-so barrels of the same age and *criadera*. This barrel will then be removed and entered into the Palo Cortado ranks, where it will be fortified and begin ageing like an Oloroso. And this is how it presents itself in the glass too. These wines tend to have the lightness and elegance of Amontillados yet notes of deep complexity like the Olorosos. They make for a very interesting drink.

But why the name? Why a cut stick? Well, this comes down to how the sherry casks are marked to identify them. Symbols are drawn onto the heads of the casks so the wines can easily be identified by which stage in the ageing process they're currently in. The symbols are written in chalk so they can easily be altered as the wine evolves over time. And here's how they go:

- The Fino gets a palm frond, basically a diagonal dash.
- Amontillado gets a little "A" with the cross section circling around it to form a halo.
- The Oloroso gets a circle with a diagonal dash through it.
- And the Palo Cortado, well we said it starts out ageing like an Amontillado/Fino right? So it starts with a diagonal dash but as it starts to evolve in its own direction it is struck with a horizontal line, thus, the cut stick.

Pretty cool huh?

And that is all (I think) I want to say about sherry. It was a lot but I got it all out. Phew.

God damn it, I'm thirsty.

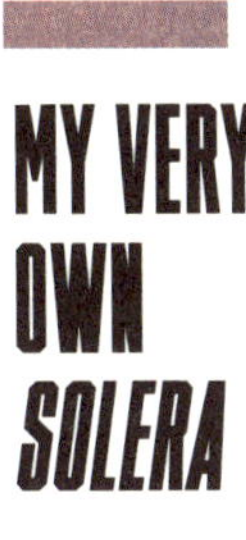

MY VERY OWN *SOLERA*

Once on a trip down south, Amy and I found ourselves in the beautiful port city of Cádiz. This city, known as the gateway to the Indias, was the Spanish door to the New World and would have been the last shimmering harbour that a lot of people saw before crossing the Atlantic. In this city, which forms a triangle with Sanlúcar de Barrameda and Jerez de la Frontera, a lot of sherry drinking goes down. But there is one place that seems to shine above the rest. Taberna La Manzanilla. This place is a real gem and a must see for those wanting to get into the nitty gritty of sherry.

"OK, so a bar," you might say. But no. It's more than that, so much more.

The joint was opened in 1932 and is now run by Pepe, the third generation of this sherry loving dynasty. In the very centre of the bar sits a stack of barrels that climb up to the ceiling, each one of them marked with the name of their contents. The bar's philosophy is all about showcasing the quality of the Manzanilla wines, the coastal sherries from the town of Sanlúcar. If you were paying attention before, you'll know.

Each year, Pepe, as his father and grandfather did before him, heads out to survey the selection. He works through a number of cellars before making his decision, selecting the very best to take back to the bar in bulk.

The wine is then used to refill the half-empty barrels so that the bar has something to serve for the year. But the fascinating part is in the detail "half-empty."

The barrels in the bar are the very same that were installed by Pepe's grandfather, and for the last 90 years that this watering hole has been open, the barrels have been forming their own unique *crianza* in what is known as a *solera estática* or static/stationary *solera*. What's more, the individual biological and atmospheric conditions of the bar and surrounding area provide a unique set of conditions, meaning a unique microbial selection. So the wines' taste is unique to that bar. Wild!

They are damn tasty too and Pepe is eager to share them and his knowledge with those who visit. So make the stop!

Have you ever heard of *vi ranci*?

The name translates from Catalan to quite literally, rancid wine. Sounds tasty no? I can assure you, it's really something.

Vi ranci is this wild tradition of sweet wine that they make from late harvest white grapes that are left swinging on these gnarly old vines late into the autumn season. Out in the jagged mountains of the Priorat where the vines cling to their steep *llicorella* terraces, and also in the *panal*-filled *fous* (the local name for the terraces that have been cut into the valleys of the region) of the Terra Alta region.

Stunning old Moscatel vines with thick trunks curling out of the soil, their grapes few but sweeter than honey and the same colour too: that glowing deep gold also tinted with a rich reddish brown. Like I say. Stunning. That was the colour of the grapes I picked that summer I worked the harvest in Catalunya. The local winery that I was picking for told me they were destined for the *vi ranci*. Once in the winery, they would take the grapes, gently destem them and set them to ferment in a cold steel tank.

They don't leave them fermenting for long, aiming to keep a fair bit of sugar. *Vi ranci* can be made with a number of different grapes but usually it's Garnacha Blanca or Moscatel for the whites and Garnacha Negra for the reds, but whatever it is, it needs to be sweet. It's after some fermentation that things get weird. They put the wine in these huge glass bottles, called *demijaunes*, or into large barrels which they then leave outside in the sun. This exposure to the elements has a profound effect on the wine, producing a sort of "thermal shock," which is apparently what kicks off the oxidising process and stabilises the wine, cutting off the activity of any microbes still hanging about. Through this process, the wine somehow enters a state of infallibility where neither time nor oxygen seem to be able to get to it. It's common these days to fortify the wine, to similar effect. The real ones, however, are left out in the sun to concentrate somewhat naturally through evaporation, achieving higher levels of alcohol and sugar.

As you can imagine, this process takes a while: a year or two spent outside at least. Then the bottles are finally allowed back indoors, where the wine is thrown into barrels, which are forgotten about for an even longer time. Some even flush the wine through a bit of a *solera* system. The wine continues to concentrate and oxidise further until developing all sorts of fun, toasted hazelnutty and almondy complexities. That's how it works in the wineries, anyway. But how do folks do it at home?

One Saturday morning in the late spring, after a run through the Terra Alta countryside, I got chatting with one of my then-neighbours. He'd heard of NZ he reckoned, but he couldn't figure out why I wanted to hang about in his small town, especially having come from so far away. He seemed pleased with the fact that I was into wine, though. His family ran one of the wineries in town, as is often the case, so he knew something of the ins-and-outs.

"If you are interested in wine, you ought to see something special. Come and have a look at this," he said, as he pulled open the large, corrugated iron door to his massive basement garage and shuffled in.

He walked into the gloom between a number of cars and different pieces of machinery before disappearing into the dark completely. That is until a little light clicked on above his head. Here, it seemed, was his stash.

Just behind where he stood in front of a little alcove that was carved out of the far side of the garage, I spied an array of dusty bottles set upon shelves that scaled the wall from floor to ceiling, some 2.5 metres (8 feet) high. He had a little bar set up there, and proceeded to pull down two small dessert wine style glasses. He then showed me the contents of a few old bottles. He had some vermút that a friend had made and a nice bit of sherry. But this wasn't what we had come to see. After a swig from his glass, his foot reached out and kicked a barrel sitting below the shelves.

"1954," he said, reading the big chalk numbers that I could see written on the face of the barrel. "The year I was born. My father bought this barrel then and filled it with *vi ranci* he made here in town."

He poured some from the tap into our glasses. "And this is what we drink on those rainy days."

"This wine is still here from 1954?" I asked, admiring the wine in my glass. Golden ochre in colour, its walnutty treacle smell dancing in my nose. It moved with a gelatinous pace across the mouth, feeling rich and complex, with a grainy sensation that tingled on the back of the tongue.

"Well sort of, but not exactly. Every year we drink a bit and then we fill it up to the top again with the winery's latest release."

That's a wonderfully long time to keep a barrel rolling with this style. *Solera estática* is the method here, and it produces some wicked results—from these "rancid" dessert wines to the world of sparkling wine. Thinking about it, I need to get me one of those old *soleras* one day. It'd be awesome to start one from scratch and see it evolve, of course, but how truly amazing to purchase a barrel that's already seen a few moons. Perhaps I can source one from Jerez and see how it adapts to Portuguese life . . .

Adding to the bucket list!

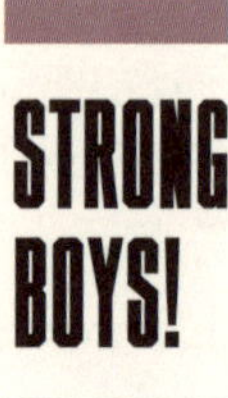

All across the Iberian Peninsula there are frequent examples of fortified wines. These wines have been incredibly popular throughout history, and I'd go as far as saying that some have even helped to shape history, having been made in these regions since forever ago. Sherry, we have already discussed. But of course, as I am sure you know, there are others. The heavy hitters being things like Moscatel, Madeira, vermouth, and port.

The term fortified simply means "made stronger," achieved by giving the wine a good kick of some local brandy, which is in turn usually made by distilling wine. The addition of this pure, wine-based spirit gives the wine a good lift in its overall alcohol content and stops any little bacteria or yeasties in their tracks. Now you have a wine that is strong, bold, and pretty solid in its state.

This concept of distillation was first introduced to Iberia by the Moors, those invaders from the north of Africa who, starting from the 8th century, came over to conquer the whole peninsula. Despite their religion of Islam restricting the consumption of alcohol, the Moors had developed tools to help them extract essential oils from plants (if you don't happen to know, many of the North African cultures remain famous for their oils and perfumes today). One of these tools in particular was the *alambique.*

An odd-looking contraption. Sort of like a lumpy gourd that is connected by a pipe to a further spiralled pipe, contained within a bucket that sits alongside. This bucket will have a little tap on the side, at the bottom of the coiled pipe. And the premise is simple. You load the raw liquid (be it alcohol, in the form of a filthy stinking wine from anything fermentable, or delightful smelling plants steeped in water) into the gourd-looking part and light a fire under its ass. This will heat the liquid, causing it to boil. The alcohol or oil, now a vapour, will rise out of the (often putrid looking) liquid and become caught in the pipe above, sending it downward through the coil. This coil will have its surrounding bucket filled with cold water, meaning the vapour will then be cooled and condensed as it passes through this cooling spiral and come out of the tap at its base as a distilled spirit or aqueous oil. (For oil-making it is then necessary to separate the oil from the water.)

This is how all spirits are still made today—from whiskey to mezcal. This also includes the brandy that they use for the fortifying, just as we saw with sherry. In Portugal and Spain they call it *aguardente* or *aguardiente*, respectively. *Agua* meaning water and *ardente/ardiente* meaning flaming or burning. You get the picture, I'm sure.

So, it is with thanks to the Moors that the Iberians have the spirits with which to fortify their wines. But why did this practice continue with such prevalence? Well, it's all to do with Iberia's relationship with the sea, that is, wanting to get across it and get good and drunk on the other side.

This part of the world has seen a lot of overseas action. Since the beginning of the Age of Discovery, the Spanish and the Portuguese (although by no means limited to) have been involved in some shady shit in every continent on the globe. And through this they encountered a massive problem. After months at sea, with highly fluctuating temperatures, when arriving in new destinations they would find their wine to be rancid. And this is not like the good shit they brew up in Catalunya either. By this I mean proper rancid. The wine would have been vinegar. I am sure you have tasted a wine that has been left out too long. It's acrid and bitter, with the vinegary hot fruit steaming up your nose as you sip it. Nasty shit. And as a result, the sailors were in need of a solution. Not just to quench their thirst and take the edge off a massive painful journey, but to turn it into gold on the foreign shores. Enter: fortification. Followed by drunken sailors the world over. I'm sure they behaved themselves.

Those are the basic Hows and Whys behind this broad category of fortified wines. However, each of these comes with their own pretty wild story, so let us not delay.

Moscatel is a funny drink, I have heard Portuguese people say a few times "Oh the Portuguese don't drink port, that is for the foreigners. We drink Moscatel."

Now, port is fascinating as well as delicious (as you will soon see), but Moscatel has some interesting points too. First off, because it's sort of like an orange wine and second, because of a rather interesting meteorological phenomenon.

So how is it orange? Well, it starts, as most wine stories do, on the vine. Moscatel is made from—you guessed it—the grape called Moscatel. It's a honeyed, perfumed grape variety that does very well when left with a touch of residual sugar. It's grown a bit in the Douro, but the good stuff comes from Setúbal, which is a little region to the south of Lisbon. Here a big plain extends south of the River Tejo until the land jolts up into the Serra da Arrábida with the sea on the other side. It's on this plain that they like to grow a load of wine grapes with which a lot of Moscatel is made.

So, these grapes are left swinging on the vine for as long as can be. They hang in there so long, in fact, that they start to dry out, which is known as *passerillage*. All that's left are these tiny, withered raisins. When they can hang on no more, they are brought inside the winery and loaded into the

tank with the skins still on as they slowly start their ferment. The fermentation goes on for about six days before they kill it with a heavy pour of *aguardente* (that same "fire water," AKA brandy). This stops the ferment in its tracks as the raised alcohol level, around 17 percent, is too high for the yeast to survive.

Now the wine is left to sit: still with all the skins intact and a lot of sugar that was not fermented out. And it stays this way for six months, after which finally the wine is pressed off the skins and left to rest in barrel for a few years. That is how they get the famous Moscatel de Setúbal, fine stuff that it is. It's got a burnt honey-brown colour to it and it's full of floral, citrus, and tea-like flavours. It slides down real easy too, the residual sugar helping out a lot.

And then there's that meteorological phenomenon I mentioned. Just when you thought we had finished with all our chats about the nature behind the wine, no no no, there's more. I am sure you're hanging on the edge of your seat.

This phenomenon is very groovy (though maybe not as epic as our buddy DIURNAL SHIFT). It goes by the name of the Föhn Effect and it is the secret behind good late harvest wines. "*Föhn*" is the German word for hairdryer, so-called because this is in effect what it does.

It comes about when there is a body of water next to a mountain range with land on the other side. The wind likes to whip around on the water side. Here it picks up lots of moisture, which cools it right down. This gust of cold, wet air is then sent towards the mountain. As it comes close to the land it is thrust upwards to the top of the mountain. Up here the temperatures drop steeply and the moisture inside the wind condenses and becomes heavy. This moisture then falls as rain on the top of the mountain, effectively emptying out the wind. Now the wind is dry and comparatively warmer. It continues to blow but heads instead down the mountain on the opposite side. The warm dry air acts like a hairdryer, aimed at whatever is growing on the far side of the mountains and thus maintaining warm, pleasant conditions for much longer than the other surrounding areas that aren't exposed to this phenomenon.

Grapes have a hard time keeping clean and healthy when the rains come and the temperatures drop. For that reason, we make sure the harvest is in and our grapes are as ripe as possible before the autumn rains arrive. However, in the areas where we have the Föhn working its magic, the grapes can hang out in the vineyard for months longer, getting crazy ripe, boosting their sugar content and eventually beginning to dry out into raisins. Dessert wine or late harvest wine is produced in a lot of regions, but with this little tip in mind, you should start to notice a lot of them have the same characteristics, especially the more famous ones.

It's this phenomenon that we see in the Setúbal region, where the waters of the Atlantic wash around the south side of the Serra da Arrábida and the city of Setúbal. The wind is pushed over this *serra* to where the vines are planted on the north side. Pretty wild, right? Although Moscatel doesn't have a colourful history of exploring the world per se, it does have a cool recipe and some epic geography behind it to boot.

So, what of those that did travel the globe? Port would be a brilliant example, having sailed to many of the world's shores . . .

What a fascinating beverage, port. Like sherry, it presents yet another bottle of worms. Once you pop one, you want to keep on poppin' every cork in sight to learn of the secrets within. There is no stopping—for me anyway.

Because these wines seem to hold the stories of times past so well. They speak of histories wherein the world was such a different place, so much further apart, so much more difficult to cross. Yet the wines were good and able to survive even the most challenging journeys. Good enough to survive the journey from then to now too. Today, we're fortunate that many of the old styles of wine are still with us. As, beyond being hella tasty, they can tell some amazing stories.

Here's the tale of port, as I've heard it told.

Again, like many of these fortified wine histories, it started with a fight or two . . . or three. From the previous stories, we know all too well that the British have always drunk the world dry, just as they continue in their attempt today. The French were being difficult as per (see: 700 years of continual fighting between the two nations), while the British were enjoying taxing the fuck out of them (as per). And don't forget the Spanish, who were of course also being difficult. Succession and Catholicism and armadas and so forth. Pettiness all around.

All of this meant wine imports (at least those of the nice n' cheap variety) were dwindling, which rather screwed things up for the average 17th-century wino on the streets of London, as you can probably imagine. This presented the Brits with a problem. And to solve it, they hoisted their sails and set their bows towards Portugal. Good relations had always prevailed between the two nations, which brought about the world's oldest continuing peace treaty, the Anglo-Portuguese Treaty of 1373. Best friends 4eva! Only issue was, in those days the Portuguese made shit wine. Or at least according to British standards. I am sure the Portuguese were fine with it (sorry again, Portugal). Historical accounts say that the wines were often heavy extractions, bitter-tasting, and the colour of crude oil. This poorer quality was accentuated by the rocky sea crossing to the UK, which would have turned to a foul stinking brew upon arrival.

The British were determined though. They knew something good must be hidden in those sunny southern lands, and so two Liverpudlians were sent down in the year of 1678 to survey the Portuguese scene, where they stayed and spent a while learning the ropes. They journeyed into the Douro Valley and surrounding regions and began shipping back whatever quality goods they could find. Their search reached a pinnacle, however, when they stumbled upon the Abbot of Lamego. This was an old monastery gig, but one where the old buggers were holding a little trick up their sleeve. The wines the men found were somehow "very agreeable, sweetish and extremely smooth," or, by my translation, pretty bomb vinho.

They were so stunned, in fact, that they purchased the whole lot and shipped it home. And to their pleasant surprise, I am sure, the wine was still pretty fucking epic when it reached the other side. See, the monks out in Lamego were cutting their fermentation short, whacking it with a dose of brandy (*aguardente* style) and leaving it to age and mature with its natural sugars and fully intact fruitiness. Needless to say, this stuff was the ticket and the UK was hooked.

And this little discovery led to some big changes. The UK started to import masses of the stuff, further spurred on by the Methuen Treaty of 1703, which brought tariffs on Portuguese imports right down. Portugal got right on board too. They figured that the area best suited for the production of this style of wine was the area of schist soils that followed the Douro River as it crossed the north of Portugal. They formed the Companhia Geral da Agricultura das Vinhas do Alto Douro (The General Agricultural Company of the Alto Douro Vineyards) in 1756 to guarantee the quality of the wines being produced and make sure the prices were kept fair. They were also in charge of regulating which wines would be good for export and which would stay in Portugal (Portugal got the shit haul again: bugger), as well as managing the protected region.

And collectively, they all agreed that the city of Porto was where the action should take place. The city, built around a harbour where the Douro River meets the ocean, was undoubtedly the best place to ship the wine from. Out in the Douro region among the vineyards, the winemakers would grow the grapes and make the wine—but how could they know what the end consumer, a thousand miles across the sea, might want? This is what led to the concept of port houses.

These houses, in truth massive warehouses, acted as headquarters for companies owned by the merchants (who themselves were usually from the countries they sold to, meaning most were British companies). These merchants would take the wine to distant shores to be sold. As such, it became standard for them to purchase the wine before having it aged and blended to their specifications in their warehouses, according to respective customers' desired style. So far so good. But wait, there was one little logistical challenge. How was the wine, made way up in the hills of the Douro region, supposed to get to the warehouses in Porto?

I guess it's lucky that they had the massive Douro River, the wine super-highway, at their disposal. It became tradition for winemakers of the Douro to build their wineries with easy access to the river, where the wine could be carried down in large barrels to boats waiting below. These boats, known as *rabelos*, were wide, flat, and barge-like, but with a sharp keel and large rudder to keep them agile as they journeyed downstream. It was no smooth sailing either. Rocks and rapids made sure of that, so it was a gamble as to whether or not the wine would actually make it. For the most part though, it made it through, sailing all the 150-or-so kilometres (90+ miles) to the city where the warehouses stood waiting.

This was the MO for port production for the next two and a half centuries. It wasn't until the middle of the 20th century that things started to change. By this point, port was not so highly coveted around the world, the river had been cut into sections by massive dams and there were functional roads and train lines to connect the city with the vines. Eventually, they even did away with the rule about port having to be produced in Porto, so now the wines can be made and aged in the Douro region too, although some makers still like to keep it real in the city, harking back to the good old days.

This is the common history of port and the one that I have come to know. But during a recent conversation with Ryan Opaz, a wine legend who provides port education classes (among many other things), I was politely informed that I was all wrong. The Vinho Verde region is apparently where our innovative monks were producing those first fateful wines, while, according to Ryan, that delicious residual sugar found in port that we know and love? That wasn't a feature of the wine until the mid-19th century. Instead, the first wines coming out of the region would probably have been more akin to dry red wines but with an extra kick from the added booze. Just when you think you know something, am I right? History, it seems, is never quite settled. Back to school for me!

Another thing. Remember how I said the wine companies were mostly British? Well, this is why a lot of the known port brands have English names. And not just the brands. All the styles have English names too. Let's have a brief look here.

The first thing to know about port is that it can take a few different directions. The big decider? Oxygen!

It should first be stated that the best ports are the oldest. Some of these suckers have been in bottle for over 150 years and they're still in top nick. The fortification holds them in place and time, with the oxygen slowly turning all that fresh jammy fruit into the smoothest old leathery caramel. It's insane.

And that is where we can start with the main styles: Ruby and Tawny.

Ruby is the fresh jam variety. These little babies have been vinified and kept free from oxygen's hands. They ferment them in a typical way, in a tank with little to no oxygen coming in contact with the wine. They cut the ferment with *aguardente*, keeping the natural sugars. Once done, it is kept in the tank, and then after a few years it is bottled up and ready for market. The flavours are super bright and juicy. There are lots of dark fruit, prune and cassis notes, and chocolatey bits too sometimes. Pretty easy and approachable drinking and, in my opinion, best served with a little chill.

Next up is Tawny port. Our shortcut to the old dusty port. This is a wine that is made much in the same style as the Ruby but when it finishes the ferment and fortification it gets loaded into the pipes, which is the name for the barrels, derived from the Portuguese name *pipa*. Here the wine sits for a good while; the minimum is five years. During this ageing the wine starts to oxidise, bringing in all the nuttiness and rich caramel notes that get deeper and more delicately complex as time passes. Because the sugar in the wine is literally caramelising to give a plethora of new character that melds together with the leathery, drying fruit.

Then you get the blends. You'll often see things like "Tawny 10 year," or 20, 30, 40, and so on. Unlike wine, with port you don't have to blend wines only of the same year. When these wines are blended for port they are a mix of all different years in order to achieve the flavour profile the winery is looking to produce. The numbers signify the average age of the blend of wines. So, a 10 year port is a little bit of 20 year, some 15, some 5, and a dash of 10. This is to create a range of different expressions at differing price points.

This stuff is all pretty good. Then we have the Mack Daddy: vintage ports are the top dog. This is where time really matters and when we see port's durability displayed—literally on the shelf. This is also why those from the 1970s, '60s, '50s, and older are not too hard to come by, with many available on the market for reasonable prices, and in prime condition no less.

A vintage port is when the wine is all from one year. It is a true expression of the vintage. To make this wine, the very best grapes on the estate (and only on the very best years) are selected and, delicately, carried into the winery. With an incredibly gentle maceration, the fruits are juiced for all they're worth to create a wine that is so very supple, elegant and complex, with a bold acidity, booming tannins, and a very rich, jammy fruit. The lively elixir is left to cool off in barrel or in tanks for a maximum of two years before it goes to bottle.

This is where some of the world's slowest and most wonderful magic comes about. The bottles are stoppered with natural cork and laid to rest in the darkest, dustiest cellar that can be found. From that point, and for the next few decades, the bottles sit with the cork taking in little swigs of oxygen. This is what brings about the gently oxidised maturation as the wine slowly glides into a state of pure, caramelised, candied cherry heaven. It's nice, OK? With some bottles, the declared proper drinking age is not for around 30 years later, sometimes more.

Whatever the style, the history of port, be it my BS or Ryan's real deal, is a fascinating one. Stemming from a group of monks (the usual suspects around here) up in the Portuguese hills (of the Vinho Verde region . . . ?) and going on to reshape the whole Douro region, the city of Porto, and the world beyond. As for the many other stories that the wines have borne witness to over centuries, in all the far corners of the world, one can only imagine.

There is another wine however, that might even have more to tell. Hailing from the little island of Madeira, it has in turn been carried pretty much everywhere!

SHIP FULL O' GOODNESS

Now, before I kick this off, I must declare something. It is something that makes me very sad and that I hope to rectify as soon as possible, which is—here goes—that I have never been to the island of Madeira. There it is. And I call myself a big fan of Iberian wine. The shame.

But wait! What I can say is that I have tried a number of them and I have read all the stories. Grab yourself a glass and I will share some of them with you.

I have heard many things about the beauty of Madeira. From what I know it is very similar to the island of Tenerife, sheer volcanic cliffs shooting high and steamy out of an angry, frothing ocean. Also like Tenerife, it is maritime and somewhat tropical, the clouds hanging heavy around its high peaks. This intense climate means to the grapes but one thing. Acidity! Yes, the island of Madeira works together with its wiry native grape varieties, their dense vines climbing over pergolas on narrow, cliffside ledges, to produce grapes teeming with sharp acidity. It is that detail right there which defines all the rest of what comes from the island and has arisen over a long and rather famous history.

As we have learned from all previous discussions about wine and history, the wines of old were usually fortified, perfect for sea journeys. And also: don't fuck with the British. That is pretty much how the story goes. At first, it was the Portuguese who got the industry going, naturally. The winemakers would fortify the wines with sugar cane spirit, like unaged rum, and have them ready for when the ships docked. They needed wine for their journeys to the East Indies—and Madeira was handily en route.

In fact, the island sat within the trade winds of many routes, so a lot of wine was sold here, both for sending across the sea and for consumption in Europe. But then there was a problem. This time, if you can believe, it didn't have anything to do with the French or the Spanish. And, if you remember correctly, the Portuguese have always been chummy with the Brits. There's only one culprit left . . .

It was the Americans! See, they'd finally decided on a little thing called Independence. They were done with the Brits. Tea in the harbour, let's have a war kind of done, right? The Brits said fine. Fisticuffs it is. Since the Navigation Acts of the 1660s, the British, under the control of King Charles II, had been slowly tightening their grip on any trade to and from the colonies, especially coming from other nations. Basically, they wanted a tax on anything that moved between Europe and the Americas. These growing restrictions slowed progress for the Americans and kind of pissed them off, as one might imagine. This, along with a whole lot of other BS with the Brits, is what eventually sparked the War of Independence 100 years later.

In all that time, though, there remained one little loophole. For some reason or other, an ink smudge or something, the island of Madeira was overlooked. King Charles had decided that Madeira should be considered part of Africa and neglected to put any block on people trading with the Americans. Needless to say, Madeira became pretty popular on US soils, most likely the only wine they could get coming from the island, and fully laden ships began to frequently make the journey. People have gone so far as to call it the first wine of America. They reckon that the old boys had Madeira present at the signing of the Declaration of Independence and that George Washington was well known to pound a few pints of it a night. The fact that they literally measured his consumption in pints really tickles me.

The journey across the Atlantic is quite a bit different to the other wine journeys up and down the western coasts of Europe. This crossing often meant around two months at sea, where a wooden hold full of wine would be heated to temperatures upwards of 40 (104 F) degrees Celsius as the sun blazed down and reflected off the ocean's surface. High temperatures would linger through the night too, the wood staying toasty all the way to America. These ships would then arrive in the harbours of Savannah, Charleston, or Wilmington and disgorge their contents. Upon tasting their newly landed cargoes the purveyors started to notice differences. The wine had deepened in its complexity and the fresh honey character had turned to this nutty caramel.

Now before you start thinking too much along the lines of sherry, think instead of *vi ranci* and the oxidative shock. The wines, subjected to all that heat, were stabilised and had begun to oxidise, developing new flavours which were all the while held together beautifully by the wines' striking acidity. This powerful acidity combined with the period of heat exposure also meant that the wines' ageability, once safely unloaded on the other side, was extreme, some might even say infinite. In a word, these wines would have been awesome. And America was awestruck.

Clearly the Americans were pleased as (Madeira-spiked) punch with their wine. But, if that's where you think the story ends, I am pleased to say it gets wilder! Picture this. Boatloads of wine were being brought into the ports of the Eastern Seaboard. The recipients would then empty out the barrels and they would be reloaded onto the ships to be returned to the island for refilling. All was going as normal. But then, one day, there was an error.

A boatload of Madeira's finest went overlooked in the hull of one of the ships as it sat anchored in the port of (um, let's say) Savannah, Georgia. For some reason or another, the wine was never unloaded and when it came time to turn heel (or rudder) and head back across the ocean, the crew must have assumed that the barrels were empty, ready to make their return for refilling. So, off they went. The wine was carried back across the sea, where, like before, it would have endured extreme temperatures for weeks on end until it reached its destination. The winemakers of Madeira must have been somewhat confused to find their precious wine once again sitting in their warehouses. Confused though they may have been, they got the glasses out. And I should imagine that they must have been pretty blown away.

The wines they were sending off across the seas would have initially been delicately floral and honey sweet. But this must have been next level. A serious "holy shit" moment occurred. The wine, now after a double journey, with twice the oxidative shock, was now even drier, more complex, and richer with its delightful notes of nutty, biscuity toffee than ever before. All of a sudden, one trip across the sea wasn't enough. They started shipping wine back and forth, back and forth. They named the wine *Vinho da Roda*—literally translating as "wine of the wheel," but in this case the meaning was more like "wine of the round trip." This became a category in itself, that the island's producers developed, sending their wine on trips around the world to seek out higher and higher qualities. In the end up to 90 percent of it would be sold in America.

And now imagine someone in the 1750s on the eastern coast of America. Again, let's say Savannah, Georgia. I've heard it's pretty. They're out for a bit of fun on a Friday night, so they nip into their local wine bar. It's hard to picture what an 18th-century wine snob would have looked like, but I'm sure they weren't too dissimilar to those of today. Anyway, at some point they're gonna lean over to you and be like, "Hey, I see you're just drinking that direct shit. Lame. Why don't you try a sip of this, it's been around the world three times, so you know it's good." There was no going back. Aside from all the back and forth going on.

Unfortunately for the Madeirans, it soon became apparent that shipping wine to and fro was pretty damn costly and it wasn't working out. It was at this point that they then began to build ship simulators in their warehouses. They figured that the wine benefitted from all that time at sea and that perhaps they could recreate it at home to save money. This led to the design of warehouses made of wood with high rafters, where they would load the wine up under the ceiling, with big open windows allowing the sun in. These rooms would get super hot during the day and cool overnight throughout the summer. In the winter they'd have a very cold rest period. The winemakers eventually came to the conclusion that after several years of ageing in these hot humid conditions, they could attain those same flavour profiles they found in their precious *vinho da roda*. This eventually replaced the shipping method and is still one of the styles in which they produce it today. What a saga, right!?

The wine is pretty cracker stuff too. Have you tried?

Although the island produces mostly red grapes of the variety Negra Mole (which is also used for madeira wine), the real steez is with the white grapes. These are used to make the top drops, each grape having its own recipe for production, putting out a range from sweet to dry. The sweetest wines are made with Malvasia; the next in line are those made from Bual—just a little bit drier. Next is Verdelho (getting drier now), 'til we get to the driest, which is Sercial. Each is achieved by varying the time between the beginning of the grapes' fermentation and the fortification, which these days is done with *aguardente* instead of the cane sugar spirit.

Some of the best wines of the island are said to be coming from the producer, Barbeito. That's what I have heard anyway. But what do I know? I have famously never been to Madeira.

Perhaps if I give them a shout out here, they'll give me the Royal Tour when I make it down there.

THE FOOT WINE

One day I had a thought as well as a burning question. When such a thing occurs, I'll often drop a line to my friend André Lourenço, the maker of many excellent wines up in the Beira region of Portugal, as we know, and someone who also possesses the power of a near instant response time at any hour.

Hey André, I poked onto the screen keyboard. *How easy is it to make a Piquette? Is it really as simple as just adding water?*

Now for those of you who aren't familiar with the term "Piquette," you clearly haven't been sippin' in the trendy wine bars where they'll make you feel bad about yourself for not knowing what a Piquette is. What it is though, is a very simple wine made with the leftover skins of the grapes. Once they have been pressed off, with the juice being taken away for the production of a standard white wine, the skins are then mixed with water and left for another fermentation. It makes a simple beverage, halfway between a beer and a wine, that's low in alcohol and even somewhat hydrating too.

But back to the conversation with André. Of course, there was an instant response.

I've tried a few times but it never seems to work. It always makes a nice vinegar though.

Not exactly what I was looking for.

Here it is called água-pé, he added.

This is a term that I had heard before, and it means foot wine or something like that.

Oh, right, I responded. *I've heard of that before. Pretty interesting story of old Portugal.*

Little did I know, that history is a little darker than that.

I'm not so sure. It's very camponês [a Portuguese word, similar to hillbilly].

Yeah? I responded, wanting to know more.

Usually the água-pé *was the beverage served to the peasants that worked the fields. It numbed the body so they couldn't feel the pain or fatigue. The good wine was for the big estate owner. The* água-pé *was a by-product.*

They were said to be able to endure backbreaking work because of the small amount of alcohol—the water content would also hydrate them til the *end of the day's work. Keeping them in that sweet spot, not drunk but relatively painless.*

Or that's how the recent story goes, he continued. *The older theory is that it was used by the ancient armies, in the Middle Ages and before. The soldiers, walking for days and days on end, were supplied with the light wine, and again before battle.*

Like the peasants, it would keep them numb. But it's for that reason it's called "água-pé"*: it was the wine that kept people on their feet. It kept them moving beyond what normal humans would be capable of.*

What a bleak history! And for something that has all the trendies in an uproar. It sure is fascinating though. History, no matter how grim, seems to have that quality. I was intrigued. How could I learn more?

I'd heard of a winemaker further up the country who had recently released an *áqua-pé*. His name is Tiago Sampaio and he produces wine in the small town of Sanfins do Douro, which sits within the demarcated Douro Valley region. This tiny town perches on the top of one of the incredibly steep and terraced hills that make this mountainous area so special. Tiago is currently producing an ever-widening array of unique and interesting wines from a broad selection of local grapes. He chooses to produce outside of the overbearing gaze of the local DO so that he can really produce the wines that the land gives him.

Among this brilliant selection, kindly laid out on a makeshift table constructed of wooden pallets, was a curious little bottle containing the *água-pé*, or as he has called it, the aqua-nat. For this he takes the skins from a load of different grapes and rehydrates them with water after the press. He claims that there is still around 5 percent of the grape's juice remaining in the skins after pressing, which is quite a lot considering those things come out like fucking cornflakes. With a little rehydration they have a bit more to give. He seems to have played around with the recipe a little over the last year or so.

Some of them have been done with white grape skins to make a sort of orangey *água-pé*. Others with a mix of red and white to make a sort of dirty rosé. In some cases, he had carbonated it with a little extra ferment in the bottle, spurred on by some added grape must. And to their one in a little bottle they added hops. I was also able to try a recent still variety out of the tank. This uncarbonated one was tangier and sourer with a floral fruity palate. Those that were carbonated or made with hops were super dry and crisp. Really floral on the nose but then pleasantly bitter on the palate. All up, they made for some pretty interesting beverages. Each was really light and easy drinking, with around 5 percent alcohol. It really is like a more hydrated form of beer, and very refreshing.

Tiago had some interesting theories on its origins too. Nowadays, wine production is so widespread and there is normal wine produced for low prices. But back in the day, when the Douro wasn't so built up and wine was scarcer, the good stuff would fetch a high price and was therefore shipped off around the world. The people at home in Portugal were poorer and either didn't have the money for the expensive wine or preferred to earn money from it, not drinking what they produced. Thus, the *água-pé* was something they could produce from the residual skins in order to have something to drink themselves.

Another theory was linked to the quality of drinking water. We are lucky to live a life of luxury these days compared to how people lived in days gone by. Water, when finally lugged into the house, was often of poor quality, contaminated with all sorts of nasty critters and not fit for consumption. And while the rich may have had their fancy pipes once indoor plumbing came along, these were often made of lead, poisoning them too. It's safe to say that clean drinking water was a scarce resource. Both at home and when travelling.

Alcoholic beverages, however, were sterilised by the presence of said alcohol, meaning that they were usually left with just the one (friendly) poison, instead of however many others that might be there. For that reason, it was common for folks in past times to consume beer, mead, or other watery alcoholic beverages in order to get their daily water needs. In places that produced wine instead of beer, the malt and barley was replaced by grape skins and a refreshing, watery, faintly grapey brew was produced.

This sheds a slightly less sinister light on the style of wine than those earlier accounts, but it is hard to know where exactly the truth lies. Perhaps it's with all of them. Whatever the story behind it, this concept of re-fermenting the skins with water seems to be a common theme in winemaking communities all over Europe and beyond, so I am sure it has seen many different uses.

It's just one more of the many ways that winemaking connects us to history. And you gotta love that!

Are you already a little bored of this chat? I am. This sulphite panic has gone on long enough.

But before I go into this, I will say that I am a fan of clean wine. Remember, clean is cool! I don't wanna drink chemical-laden shit that barely passes as fit for consumption, loaded with enough sulphites to kill a horse. There is a lot of that crap about. In fact, it's the majority, and I'm not into it. I am pretty into all things environmental, so the wines I work with, as well as the ones I like to sip, are of the natural or low intervention (lo-fi) variety. The ones I like to sip, that is. Sometimes you inevitably find yourself at an underground rave in some disused warehouse refilling beer bottles with acrid boxed wine. What I am trying to say is, life is about balance.

I am into the lo-fi stuff as I believe the environment needs our protection and it, sort of, seems worth the effort. If you're not yet convinced, please return to the start of the book and read again. I'll meet you back here. Because alongside the wonderful nature that seeds these kinds of wines, the dedication, time, and energy that their producers put into them, and in an ever more sustainable fashion, is impressive and humbling. They are good people to support. It's just that I start to get a little bit jaded when listening to the never-ending sulphite debate.

So, what is it all about?

Well, sulphites are a group of sulphur compounds, most of the time by-products of the petrochemical industry (ugly) and used in winemaking to stop the microbes in the wine from doing more stuff. This "more stuff" is what can alter the quality of the wine and turn it into a hot stinking mess. Sometimes it's the wrong yeasts multiplying, like with *Brettanomyces* or whoever else is in there mixing up the brew and destabilising things to bring about volatile acids and the like. There's also the oxidation element that sulphites work to prevent (sorry, sherry). It can be kind of gross, mousiness being the worst outcome. If you know you know (*wretches*); if you don't stay tuned.

I once heard sulphites' effect described in an interesting way: "The sulphites work like a camera. They take a snapshot of a moment in time and preserve it there." It's a curious way to think about it. The microbes have done their bit and now we need them to take a backseat to preserve this creation in its best form. This is why sulphites can be good.

But then there is the wave of militant anti-sulphite winemakers and natty wine enthusiasts. They get rather heated about it. It kills the wine, they say. The wine should dance and be alive and so on, and they vehemently swear to never put it in theirs. I get it; wine without sulphites is a good concept, especially when considering where it comes from. Wine without any additions sounds awesome. It's just not all that simple though. The wine has to taste good. This is the bit that gets me. Natural is only cool if it tastes good, in my opinion. Oh, what about this one, the one that tastes like a sweaty, flatulent onion? Na, I'm fine without.

There are some wonderful wizards and witches out there in this world, making some incredible, magical potions, where they achieve this perfect harmony and balance in their vineyards which they transmit to their wine. It's remarkable. But then there are a number (the cowboy winemakers I refer to) who proudly announce their complete disuse of sulphites as they thrust their putrid concoction in your direction. If you can go without, great, but don't fuck your product just to please the label.

Often it is the case that the sulphites make the difference. It's their responsibility to get it from the winery all the way to the drinker's glass (on whatever face of the world that might be) in just the condition that it was initially intended to be in. People swear down that the addition of sulphites has a marked effect on taste too, the wines being so much more "alive" in its absence—whether you think that is good or bad. While some have even described a tightness they feel at the back of the throat brought on when there is an excessive amount added. I'm all for the reduction of sulphite use—they definitely shouldn't be needlessly piled in there—but then sulphites also naturally occur in the grapes, so . . . a sulphite-free wine is technically impossible. But how much really screws the pooch?

I have come to know a number of producers who strive to keep their intervention as minimal as possible. Sometimes they attain this, other times they have to add a little something along the way to keep things clean and stable. No shame there. It is better for them to put out a quality product that can be enjoyed by all than to hold off on this addition and leave it up to chance.

All this is before we mention the hordes of sulphite haters that follow along behind these non-sulphitist leaders. They are mad too. Though for entirely other reasons. It has become the craze to drink wines without sulphites, it seems. It's the buzz word thrown around at parties or snooty wine bars. It is very on trend and people are just gagging to throw it into conversation somewhere. Furthermore, like skimmed milk or diet coke, it has supposedly made wine healthier???

"Sulphites are the real killer, man, they just ruin the wine experience for me."

Or worse.

"I just can't drink wine with sulphites. I have a huge headache the next day.'"

No, Janet, drinking four bottles of wine by the pool gave you a headache. Wine is a diuretic. It dries you out and gives you a hangover, natural or not.

There are of course those who have a real sensitivity, but the hot flashes to full-blown hives are a little different to getting a hangover. Also, a bag of chips or some dried apricots will have way more sulphites than wine, so if that doesn't knock you out, some sulphites in your glass ain't gonna do too much harm. It's improbable that you have a sulphite allergy, but they have become the top target regardless. And as a result, people are ganging up to get rid of them. "Natural is best," they say, or "Do you have any zero-zero wines?" (AKA zero additives in both the winery and vineyards).

There have been new studies that have come to light, however. All of a sudden there is confusion. And the cause of it all? Histamines. These are what is known as Biogenic Amines. Protein chains that occur and in some cases form in the wine. These are the same folks that get you all snuffly in the springtime. Well, they've been found to be in wine too. Furthermore, they're finding that these are more likely the culprits for all the headaches (all the legitimate, non-hangover ones, anyway). And what is most interesting, it's often the more natural wines that contain higher levels of histamines: sulphites and high acidity being the thing that tends to lower their count in a wine.

So where the fuck does that leave all us sulphite haters now!? It might be possible that, just like with low-fat milk, we've been angry at the wrong guy this whole time. That's my take anyway. Do with it what you will, but now you at least know that there might be someone else out there responsible for your headaches, and it might be that after all that bitching and moaning about sulphites we're living through that it's actually the wines of the natural variety which are more headache-inducing. Shucks!

If you want to create a wine without sulphites, be my guest. But let's cut the applause when the wine tastes like shit—maybe it was better off as vinegar anyway. On the chance that it does taste great: well done, miraculous, applause to you. Also, genuinely thank you for your contribution to preserving the environment and lowering our consumption of a petrochem by-product. If you are a seasoned pro and make your wine in a very conscious way, always working to the minimum of intervention but with the understanding that some interventions are on occasion necessary to hold your creation together, then I think that is also great.

And for those drinkers out there who are still getting a kick out of all this sulphite hating, just make sure you have the right enemy. Drink lo-fi wines if it makes you happy and do your bit for the environment that way. Just remember that sulphites, or a lack of them, are not going to make all your dreams come true.

FLOWER POWER

OK, maybe I don't give too much of a fuck about the sulphites in my wine. I want them kept to a minimum, sure, but I understand that sometimes you have to put them in. Especially when you wanna send it far and wide across the world to sate the thirsts of distant lands.

What's not cool though? That shit is a by-product of the fossil fuel industry!? Producers are doing so much to make their impact as small as possible only to be cut short at the final hurdle by an unavoidable ingredient that is mined in environmental hell. And then there's me as the consumer. The last thing I want on my conscience is to know that the one "chemical" which went into my wine is linked up to the world's biggest polluters.

(*Internal Earth warrior screams.*)

But what if there was another way? There's a quiet movement that little by little is starting to take hold around the natural wine scene, especially here in Portugal. It all started in a small village in the north. The charge is being led by a man named Fernando Paiva. This guy is a legend. I have had the pleasure of meeting him at a wine fair once upon a time in Lisbon and it was great to hear him talk about his work. He is one of the first producers in Portugal to be officially biodynamic and he has been setting the scene straight for a long time. He makes wine under the label Quinta da Palmirinha—a vibrant selection of zingy wines that he produces in the Vinho Verde region in the north of Portugal. Fernando does and has done a lot of cool things to advance the message of clean production in the wine industry here in Portugal—but now he is really onto something big!

It is believed that the first inkling of this came from local cheesemakers. To cure and preserve their cheese, they were using flowers from their chestnut trees, which they would dry and rub into the cheese's exterior. This seemed to work quite nicely for the cheese, which got Fernando thinking about his wine. With the help of a local university, he started to experiment using the chestnut flowers that grew abundantly on his property. At first it was with just 100 litres (about 26 gallons) or so. The following year a full tank. Now he is producing all his wine with the use of these flowers and the trend is catching on like wildfire.

It turns out that the chestnut flowers, known by the scientific name of *Castanea sativa*, and which grow on massive trees in great abundance across much of Portugal, have something of a preservative effect. When added to the wine they are said to be antioxidant and antimicrobial, with stabilising properties. Much like the discovery that added hops would better preserve beer on its journey to India (look up the history of Indian Pale Ale if you don't know what I am talking about—this is a fuckin' wine book), these chestnut flowers are proving that they can do the work to stabilise the wine and keep the yeasties and other microbes from funking shit up.

I have now met with a number of winemakers who are using or experimenting with this method. On a recent trip through the Vinho Verde region, Amy and I chanced upon a young producer, Fausto, who, well-versed in the ways of regenerative farming and agroforestry, was trying his hand at a little winemaking. In his makeshift winery, constructed among the vines on his lush, green patch of land, he was fermenting a few batches of grapes. The stems of the chestnut flowers he had also harvested from his land now littered the ground outside. He reckoned it took about a kilogram (a little over 2 pounds) of the fine, powdery petals and pollen (which can be easily separated from the flower's stems) to stabilise 1000 litres (264 gallons) of wine. Not just this, but the flowers are able to handle this workload and give zero flavour to the wine. And did I mention that they grow fucking everywhere!?

This is a huge revelation for the wine world that has the potential to change things down to the very foundation and it is so exciting to see it. Already, a company in the north of Portugal known as Tree Flower Solutions has taken up the opportunity, making themselves the first (that I know of) company to be commercialising these flowers as a product for winemakers.

Exciting times, people. Exciting times!

So, with this discovery, perhaps it is possible to have our cake and drink it too. Wines can now reliably be made in a way that is natural and ecological, whilst being able to withstand the challenges that a global wine market throws at them. For all those that hate sulphites, because their mate's mum was told by her hairdresser that they give you a headache or whatever reason, I still say it's time to move on.

Armed with this information, however, I wonder what the anti-sulphitist winemaking crowd will do with it.

DOs AND OTHER GOVERNMENTAL FUCK UPS

The whole deal with DOs is a long chat. In theory they do some good, I suppose. What they are ostensibly all about is protecting what's uniquely theirs and making it the best it can be. But do they actually do that?

Denomination of Origin or DO (it might have a different acronym in other countries) is a term that relates to the governing body of a wine region. These guys are the bureaucrats that decide which grapes are allowed, what the wine styles will be, how much oak to use, where the "border" sits and, most annoyingly for some, whether you're even allowed to put the town where the wine was made in on the fucking label. The concept here is that they promote quality in the region and make sure that whatever goes out into the world under that name tastes good and is made the classic way with the real local shizz.

Perhaps in some ways they do a good job, and even a necessary job, but I only really get to hear about the negative side. More or less every winemaker I have ever met has had a run in with the local wine authorities at some point, regarding something they have made that doesn't comply with regulations. It usually results in the producer losing a lot of money, having to reprint the labels or flog the product off as bulk wine—all because the pen pushers aren't happy.

I guess one positive might be the restriction around foreign grape varieties entering the area. It would be a crying shame to see all the indigenous varieties ripped up in favour of the more popular Cabernets and Chardonnays and such. But then it's these same regulatory bodies that have enforced ideas like Californication in the first place, a measure that for the most part has stripped the region of its true identity. DOs ultimately seem to always follow the money too, working to support the big players while leaving the smaller producers in a sort of DO-or-die position.

Thankfully, it does seem as though things are moving away from all of this now. For years, there have been whispers of rebel winemakers who have ditched the DOs in favour of doing whatever they damn well please. These guys are the natural, lo-fi or experimental crowd that want to do things differently and work to their own philosophies. They don't seek to conform and they certainly don't care for barrel-ageing the living daylights out of their wine in order to get the fancy sticker. What's more is that it's usually this crew that is preserving the local authenticity best. Farming in ways that protect the local environment and terroir and working with the indigenous varieties. For the most part, these regulatory bodies do nothing to encourage a more sustainable and clean method of wine production. But this new crew are emerging as the heroes of their respective regions, and consumers all around the world are excited to try their stuff. The wines they're producing, which are of exceptional quality and brilliantly unique, are nowadays less likely to be shunned, nor refused the right to say where they were produced.

The DOs seem to be a bit of a dinosaur in the modern wine world. On top of this, there has been an emergence of alternative regulatory bodies which seek to regulate quality and give less of a fuck about the source, style, and grape variety. So perhaps we will soon see the extinction of the DOs. I, for one, am nonplussed. I don't need the government's help in telling me which wine is good and proper and which is "not." Right? And after reading all this shit I've written neither do you. Right??

It brings to my mind the art of Picasso and his struggles against Franco's fascist regime in Spain. The politicos did their best to do away with him as he continued to make art that exposed them, which eventually led to his exile in France. And who came out on top in the end? What I mean to say is, just like with some of the beautiful wines out there today, the art was great but the gov' couldn't handle it.

Anyway, we're gonna find all them epic wines and drink 'em regardless.

Keep on fighting the good fight.

One such place where the BS efforts of a biased regulatory body are painfully clear is in the small town of La Seca, near Valladolid, Spain. This area has some wicked terroir. As you should well know by now, this part of the country is on a high altitude plain that slopes down to the Duero River. On these plains are these massive limestone pebbles the size of a fist, if not bigger, while below and among them the soil is loose and sandy.

This is prime territory for white wine production as there's free draining soil, the days are scorching hot, with the flat plain heating up like a frying pan, and the nights get hella chilly (DIURNAL SHIFT!!!). With everything so exposed, the heat has nowhere to hide. The area produces wines with lots of crunchy acidity, bright floral aroma, and wonderful minerality. For this reason, the grape Verdejo evolved here, showcasing exactly that. But now, it seems, only that. Verdejo is the only thing that can be produced here and only in one particular style (if you want the wines registered with the local DO, that is).

So, what went down?

My guess is that the Spanish wine industry was threatened and/or jealous of the rise in popularity on the world market of the zingy summer sippers made from Sauvignon Blanc and Pinot Grigio. They saw what was happening and also their opportunity to get in on the action. Their cash cow would be none other than Verdejo and they laid down the law in the Verdejo capital, Rueda, decreeing that only steel-fermented, unaged, high acidity wines could be made with it. Supermarket fillers, basically. Cheap to produce and easily scalable to produce massive quantities. And today, this is the state in which Verdejo is found all over the world.

This is all I ever knew of it, too. All throughout my time living in Spain there would often be some Verdejo on offer at a party or an open bottle on a restaurant table (never me who ordered it, just FYI). If there was nothing else, I might take a dash, but it wouldn't ever be too pleasing. Generally, it would come across like water with a lime squeezed in it. Nothing but sharp acidity and . . . yeah, that's about it. So, I started to shun it. Not for me, thanks. That is until I came across the wines of a few breakaways in the town of La Seca. These were unlike any others I had ever tried and to say I was intrigued was an understatement. I had to make a trip!

Amy and I tripped over to Madrid from Lisbon and, after cruising through La Rioja for a few days, we followed the roads down to La Seca, where Beatriz Herranz and Félix Crespo of Barco del Corneta had agreed to meet me. They greeted us warmly and welcomed us into their winery. Beatriz, the OG founder, along with Félix and the crew have been working the vines and making wines in the area since 2010 and they are doing things a little differently.

In fact, I was completely unaware until our visit that not only are they making their wines differently, the place in which they do so is rather unique too. After a look around and a quick chat we descended. Two storeys below their winery we were faced with a long tunnel that stretched off into the distance.

"The whole subterrain of the town is a labyrinth of tunnels like this," Beatriz informed us. "They were dug around 200 years ago and provide us with optimal storage conditions for ageing wine."

The tunnels maintain a stable temperature and humidity, unlike the fluctuating plains above, so it's the best place for the barrels. And it's here that they are working with the grape Verdejo, same as everyone else in the area, but instead of the usual, they are ageing it in oak barrels. And compared to the usual Verdejos, which are just soulless acidity, these wines are rich and complex. They burst with melon, lemon rind, and this herby, fresh-cut grass sort of note. The acidity moves long and slow with a honey-like ooze but then sharpens up just in time to freshen the complex mineral depth that lingers in the mouth.

The wines are delicious basically, and unlike any Verdejo you will ever find. They are an incredible example of both what the area can produce and what some very talented winemakers can do. But as you may have guessed, these wines are not accepted by the local DO. Instead, the labels carry the sticker of the greater region, Castilla-Leon, a much more liberal wine authority.

It is a classic example of a regulatory body fucking shit up with their carefully branded crap. The question is though, should we be angry? Or should we just say, "Fuck your DOs!"?

THE WORST WINE IN THE WORLD

The Dão region of Portugal sits in the centre of the country, just to the south of the mighty Douro River. The region is essentially a plateau that gradually drifts up into the Serra da Estrela, the highest mountain range on the mainland. Its soils are loaded with granite, as are its mountains—with towering granite pillars stabbing out of their peaks. The vineyards are high here too, between 400 and 600 metres (between 1300 and 2000 feet) above sea level. The mountains to the south and east shield it from the hot heats that drift over from the Spanish plains in the east. And then in the west sits the Atlantic, although the region is also slightly separated from the coast. This is due to another smaller mountain range called the Serra do Caramulo. So, all of this to say, the Dão has got its own little climate, with a fair bit of DIURNAL SHIFT caused by the altitude. As a result, the wines it produces are crisp with bold structure and wonderful complexity.

But it wasn't always the case. Dão has had some dark times. There was a period through the middle of the 20th century, starting in 1932, where

Portugal was ruled by the fascist dictator António de Oliveira Salazar. He was, for the most part, pretty fascist, as the description may suggest, but then he went and did something sort of communist.

The Dão region, being a rocky and wild terrain, never used to be so well connected to the rest of the country. Therefore big business was scarce and the majority of agriculture was subsistence farming, that is. everyone produced just what they needed. This is the way it went for wine too, with each household growing and bottling just enough wine each year to sate their family's thirst. But then Salazar came along, who was ironically from the Dão and owned vineyards there throughout his life, and decided that the region needed more wine production, for consumption within the country (he wasn't a fan of exports). To solve this he made a rule that private wineries could not buy other farmers' grapes and had to use only their own produce to make their wines. Any other grapes that were produced had to be sold to one of ten cooperatives that were built in the region.

But here's the problem: the co-ops, which were owned collectively by all those who participated, paid for quantity and not quality. Farmers were thus incentivised to load up any old shit into the tractor for payday when the harvest rolled around. This in the best case included grapes, and even these were often at extremely varied stages of ripeness. There were also the stones and other such things that people would sneak into the baskets to weigh things down. Stones are great in the vineyards (see the section on terroir) but shit when they're in the wine.

Time went on, and the wines got continually worse until the 1980s, by which point Dão was well known for utter crap. These were mashed up, prolonged macerations with all the stalks and stems, then barrel-aged to fuck to produce wines with all the consistency and elegance of motor oil. The wine legend Jancis Robinson once described them as some of the toughest, hollowest, most uncharming wines in the world.

Luckily, this was not to be the case forever. With the passing of this dictator and the EU bringing reform to the wine scene there was hope again. A number of winemakers knew Dão for the wines of old—wines of spectacular quality—and as things loosened up these producers started work returning the region to its former glory. Names such as João Tavares de

Pina, Antonio Madeira, and Alvaro Castro are just a few. Nowadays, you sometimes see producers put "Dão" in large letters on their bottles as a form of protest, so that everyone will know where the beautiful wine they are drinking comes from.

And it really is beautiful. This privileged terroir, sitting high on its own plateau, may just be the best the country has to offer. So let's keep it free of meddling bureaucrats and keep the stunning wine free-flowing.

Saúde!

A FORCE FOR GOOD

Just when you think you know something you realise you know nothing at all. That often happens to me anyway. I guess that's the beauty of wine and the wonder of the world.

One such revelation occurred when I was invited to discover more about the Wines of Alentejo Sustainability Programme (AKA the WASP). I'll have to say, I was sceptical. In past experience, a visit to the DO's club rooms to talk about sustainability involved some form of puppet with a (corporate winery-owned) gun in their back talking about how they recycled some boxes last year. I am very pleased to say that in this case I was wrong. In fact, I left with a feeling of inspiration.

The WASP initiative is led by a guy called João Barroso. He is a sustainable engineer with no real (or at least prior) wine knowledge, who came along in 2015 to lead the sustainability charge. "Sustainability" is a convoluted word that is mixed up with too much bullshit, similar to "natural wine," and it was intriguing to hear from João in his opening sentences that he is pretty firmly against any greenwashing. Which is a good thing too, considering the EU is attempting to ban it now, where they can expose it. What João is for, and doing, is something that I thought was pretty unique and special.

He said he derived a lot of inspiration from similar programmes in California and Chile (so credit to them too) when he started to look at ways to get people behind methods of better and cleaner practice. Essentially, what he has created is a cool kids club that is free to join and relatively easy to begin implementing. This more sustainable method for wineries is laid out in 18 chapters that detail exactly how to be positively impactful in the way that you produce. These chapters include the obvious, like soil management, water consumption, and chemical use, but also things like human resource management, which looks to improve the social and economic sustainability of the industry. Once your winery complies with 80 percent of the chapters you are eligible for a plaque to hang in your winery, in the vineyards, and also display on your bottle's label.

And the truly brilliant thing is: it seems to be working. The first ones to partake in the programme started to display these little plaques about the place and from there, more and more folks wanted in. Starting from 20 or so members in 2015 when they first launched the initiative to over 600 in 2022, WASP is one of the leading sustainability programmes in the world. Not just that, but they have now come to see its economic value: it is creating jobs and revenue. People are getting hired at the bigger wineries just to manage the WASP procedures. And the markets are starting to respond.

Grapes produced under WASP supervision are fetching 5 to 10 percent more when sold, while the finished wines, complete with their little emblem, are now pulling higher prices too. Maybe I am wrong and the DOs can make a positive difference—if applied in the right way. It certainly seems to be on the agenda here in the Alentejo and I am very excited to see how it progresses.

In the previous section I mentioned a few of the different and better ways in which we can produce our grapes. But I didn't share many of the cold hard facts. Filipa Silva from Quinta da Costa Pinhão in the Douro has been kind enough to share a few of them with me that I am now able to pass onto you. Wine production can be something of an ugly business when the spotlight is shone on it. Like when comparing the amount of chemicals needed to conventionally produce one tonne of grapes with one tonne of corn. Corn requires 40 kilograms (88 pounds) of agrochemicals while grapes require 50 to 100 (110 to 220). Where corn requires 22 litres (nearly

6 gallons) of fuel for the machinery used, grapes require 130 litres (more than 34 gallons). And on top of that, there is a fuck tonne of water consumption, as well as another metric fuck tonne of carbon emitted during and after production for things like electricity use, transportation, and packaging.

The world of wine is not all pretty vineyard visits and something nice to swill and suck back. In fact, it's pretty nasty when presented with these facts: remember this all affects you too. That is why it is so incredibly refreshing to come across sustainability programmes that actually seem to be making a difference instead of just the necessary noise to make you think that they are.

I hope this kind of outlook will soon be adapted by more regions around the world (apply pressure if you can!) and we can all see a reduction in those figures stated above.

BREAKING: NATURAL WINE NOW TASTES GOOD

Natural wine entered the scene with a bang. I mean quite literally. The volatile acidity in half of these drops means the wine leads with a sour fruit kick, which blasts your mouth to bits and then vanishes before it's halfway down the tongue. And there's a whole subset of wine drinkers out there who understandably fear this fizzle and pop, akin as it is to a disappointing firecracker, and think it's what defines this style of winemaking. What was initially intended as an eco-conscious alternative to mass-produced, soulless table wine has now evolved in many consumers' eyes to signify wine that is riddled with faults, with these being mischaracterised as "individual characteristics."

I've drunk a lot of wine. I've served a lot of wine. And in recent years I've seen an onslaught of eager drinkers coming to the bar asking for the natural stuff. When I ask what kind of wine they enjoy or what flavour profile they're looking for, they answer, "You know, natural and funky." Or worse, they might tell me things like, "This wine doesn't taste very natural." Natural winemaking isn't a flavour, it's a method, as I hope this book has demonstrated to you. But the market has been completely saturated and thus defined by the cowboy winemakers who make something that is weird and wild but isn't really . . . well, wine.

It started as a philosophy. One that would see the removal of all the harsh and nasty chemicals from the process and get us back to drinking the pure wines of old. This means no -cides in the vineyards and no sly additions to cover one's ass in the winery. A little sulphur is sometimes OK, but it depends who you are talking to. Upon reaching the mainstage however, it quickly became synonymous with wild experimentation that neglected the requirement of good quality. These are wines that have no regulatory body either, no one to say for certain that they were produced in any one way or another. We may not love the DOs, but in some cases we may need them (or some variation of). As it stands today, one can take any grapes, even those produced with the most chemicals out there, and ferment them without added yeast or chemicals, such as sulphites, and use this "natural" label. It's a tale as old as time: style overtaking substance, founding philosophies swapped out for profit. You know how it goes.

The term "natural" or *sans souffre* was brandished as a way to describe such wines and waved around like a trophy at a football stadium amidst much fanfare, while the wine itself, forgotten in the background, continued to cast off putrid odours as it descends to a mousy acrid death. The common practice here (or lack thereof) seems characterised simply by the abandonment of each ferment to its unregulated fate, after which all attending its product then proceed, between chokes and grimaces, to feign their enjoyment of it. Funky!

But this is not what wine is.

Wine is a beautiful piece of art, a true marriage of the terroir and unique craftsmanship. The way it caresses the tongue and fills the mouth with bursts of wonderfully shaped and nuanced flavours, the elegance, the acidity, complexity, and delicate softness. It can be one hell of a jaw-on-the-floor experience. That's why I can't help but feel a little cheated when, with excitement building, the server approaches the table, pops the cork, and serves me up a glass of tangy, eggy, dishwater. If I was in the mood for a Belgian sour beer, this would hit the spot. I ordered a wine, though.

But I do want a clean wine. I'm a conscious consumer and the planet's health is at the top of my mind. You might think this puts me at a crossroads: mass-market chemical poison or disastrous, experimental natural wines. Thankfully, there's another option. Classic styles, made with classic quality. Decades before the words "natty wine" ever graced the lips of the Brooklyn hipster, there has been a quiet army of skilled, principled wine producers who are passionate about working in harmony with the earth and putting out complex wines of exceptional quality. These are the ones I've referred to as the "rebel winemakers." They're the winemakers that are looking to express the terroir in its purest form, working with what nature gives them and making it shine.

A natural wine still needs to be nurtured. The chemical intervention in these wines is still as low as possible but there is a degree of skill and know-how involved, meaning this style of winemaking is as technical as any other. I'd liken the method with which they produce their wine as comparable to how naturopaths work to cure the ailments of the natural body, while the more conventional winemaker works more similarly to a regular GP.

They stretch the imagination too, for in this world there are no norms. They'll take a famous grape, like Verdejo, but instead of underestimating it, using a bland ferment amounting to a shock of acidity that primes it for homogenous high volumes, they'll age it. Or in the lands of volcanoes, where flinty, matchstick notes are a common feature due to that volcanic reduction we discussed earlier, they'll strive to integrate it into the wine instead of simply chemical bombing the liquid clean of its individuality. The old industry winemakers are baffled by this deviation from the norm, but the experimental drinkers are blown away by its fullness of flavour and its incredible uniqueness while still showing all the marks of quality.

These wine producers also have an ingrained sense of respect for the environment, one that's not contrived from a marketing seminar on What Millennial Drinkers Want. They are excited about finding better ways to grow grapes and produce wine in a way that gives as much back to the earth as it takes. They are not only the reproducers of the terroir, but they are its protectors, who will ensure it is here for generations to come. *This* is the future of natural wine. It's minimal intervention; it's led by standards of excellence for both the environment and the end-product. They're not afraid of a touch of sulphur to preserve the balance and know that a little temperature control to keep the fruit clean is not a sin. The result is wine with as much eye-opening potential as the age-old beloved classics, but with more vigour, vitality, and individual expression than ever before. It's farming according to the principles of land preservation too, keeping the terroir fertile and healthy for generations to come.

The natural movement has added a few tricks, though, which shouldn't be ignored. The first of these is the liberal use of skin maceration with whites. Orange wines can be incredible—but so can anything on that spectrum. Even just a touch of cold-soak maceration to pull out more aroma and unctuosity can work wonders. And as these methods are becoming more popular, the quality is on the rise, along with diversity. This use of maceration extends into the rosé camp too, where there is a lot more experimentation coming out among heavier styles, such as lighter reds.

Back in the day, there were reds and there were whites and nothing in between. The world is open now, thanks to the natty wine movement, and we are free to enjoy an enormously wide range of styles as the spectrum stretches in both directions. Pet nat too, when the bubbles are produced in the wine as it finishes its ferment in the bottle, is a style that is a lot of fun and when done right produces real quality. Thanks again to the natty wine buzz, this is another one that we'll be seeing more of on the main stage.

On the whole, this represents a general movement away from the homogeneity demanded by a globalised market and towards production that embodies the true identity of each and every parcel of land. This shift, if not entirely due to the natural wine movement, has certainly been helped along by it. And as I said, it is an exciting time for the wine world. It all seems to be unifying: there's the one party who wants good, clean, happy-Earth wine, and there is the other who wants the full wine experience with stunning quality and characteristics. They're coming together now and the future is looking bright! It's also looking pretty natural, something which may disappoint some. But to those in that squad, I can reassure you that there is a lot to look forward to. The best is still to come.

Let's all drink to a "natural" future, because it's going to taste great!

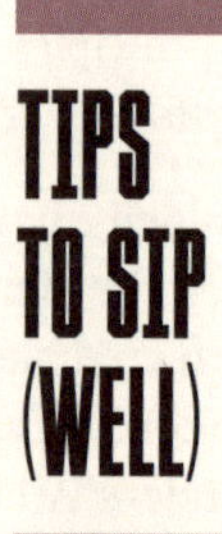

We did it! We got to the end. That was a lot . . . OK fine, we're *nearly* at the end. There's still just a little drop more to add. How about some actually actionable advice on how to drink better? How to find that bomb vinho! As we can see from the journey we've just been on together, there is no single answer to this question. The world is just too big and great and full of variety.

And let's be honest—isn't it fantastic that it is this way? Minus all the myriad factors that go into making brilliant wines it'd be a pretty boring subject. I for one am more than certain that I wouldn't have this great love in my life without the stories behind them. I mean, how many people do you know that are passionate about soft drinks? Something manufactured, artificial, and homogenous, compared to the amount that you know who love their wine? It's not comparable, in fact. So, I want to give thanks again to our wonderfully diverse and dynamic world and to all those attempting to capture their small part of it in each bottle they put out.

But now we know it's out there . . .

How do we get at it? My top tip is always just to be adventurous. If you can't pronounce it or have never heard of it, chances are there is something more exciting in there than the one you know or recognise. Be brave, take a risk, and try that bizarre thing. And hey, if it doesn't go exactly as you would have liked, you're still just as drunk as you would have been with the perfect wine, so that's nice. Then try, try again.

I more often than not find that this works in my favour. When considering conventional, DO-approved wines in particular, siding with the lesser-known variety, region, or country over the more popular at the same price point lands me with a better quality and more interesting wine. This all comes down to the relative prices for quality grapes: for the better-known regions, often the grapes have a higher market value, so they won't be using the good stuff for a moderately priced bottle. That means the quality of a 10 euro bottle from the lesser-known variety/region/country is most likely going to be higher than from the famous one.

With the whole movement around natural wine stirring up a lot of confusion this obviously becomes a little difficult. There are still a lot of cowboys out there charging top dollar for absolute shit. It can make the task of choosing a little more challenging. That is perhaps why this next tip is all the more important.

The second tip (if you're into it) is to be curious.

Take each time you drink a wine as an opportunity to learn and you will find this wondrous adventure unfolding in front of you. When I say be curious, what I mean is talk to people, for example the guy selling the wine (this is why it's always best to buy wine from your small local purveyor too) or, for those with social anxiety, even just look it up online. Computers are glued to the end of every fingertip these days and can shine more light onto what each bottle contains. I tend to avoid the apps where everyone can vote; these are too subjective and not always contributed to by the more informed crowd (i.e., wine professionals). Also, even the scores given by the professional reviewers are constantly coming under fire for their bias or conflict of interest. It's a tough world. Look instead at the websites and social media pages of the producers and read their messages. Also, those selling from their independent (online) shop will often have good info.

If, like me, you're into the cleaner side of production, it is best to look beyond the standard marketing of We Love Our Land or other generic winery bullshit and look for the hard evidence. Those doing things in a clean way will have all the information on their websites, or at the very least, they will have some photos uploaded of their processes in action. They have nothing to hide and so wear it with pride. Those that are ambiguous about what they do and how they make it are always covering up some shady shit.

And if you're tired of the natural wine style (funky, fizzy, slimy . . .), my best rule of thumb is to avoid the ones who broadcast their "naturalness" too much. Those making magic in a clean way tend to have a subtler approach to communicating their clean processes. After all, they are still believers in and scholars of the wine world who want to preserve it as they know it, in a way that also gives back to our Mother Nature. This is where terms like low-intervention, minimal intervention, and lo-fi—as well as our clean farming terms—come in handy. They have come to define the classic styles of quality but made with environmentally conscious methods.

I sincerely hope that what I have imparted here has been of use and will encourage you to drink many stunning wines from many foreign shores. Especially if those shores are Iberian.

Although I guess I should make quick mention of how to know what's up or what to do when things go wrong. We all know how the world works and we know that not everything can be perfect every time. If only you're just learning that here now, you probably need a different book. This applies to wine as well: sadly, sometimes the best of bottles just don't make it across the finish line.

Here is a quick list of what to watch out for:

The first one would be cork taint. The cork industry has done a lot of work to ensure the quality of their corks, up as they are against some stiff competition (screw caps and alternative packaging) in recent years. Not every cork can be perfect, however, and this will manifest as an earthy, damp, wet basement or wet cardboard stank in the wine. Best to send that bottle back.

But what if the wine is tasting and smelling metallic or plasticky? A nice bouquet of Band-Aid. Well, this is known as "reduction." They say it is the result of not enough oxygen being available to the wine, but it seems due more to sulphur compounds that have built up in the wine. This is fairly common when the wines are young and coming straight out of a tank or other large vessel, but one would hope it's not still like that when coming out of a bottle. If it is, it might just need a little spin and shake about. Perhaps give it a minute to catch its breath.

That plastic smell could also be attributed to another stinker that goes by the name of *Brettanomyces* or *Brett* for short. This guy is a pretty common yeast but he can cause a bit of a stink if he gets into the wine and multiplies. Some winemakers encourage it a little as it can bring more roundness and texture to those leathery, mushroomy, or even manure notes (yes, this can be a positive thing) in the wine. The Priorat is one place that this goes down on occasion, where there is sometimes a tradition of minimal cleaning for the barrels which encourages a bit of this yeast. In small quantities it can be OK but left unchecked it can turn the whole wine into a stinking mess of animal, barnyard, sweaty saddle, metallic, or plastic flavours and aromas. One to watch out for, especially when there are few sulphites thrown into the brew.

There is another one that you really must be on the lookout for and that is mousiness. This is when the wine smells and tastes like a dirty mouse cage. You know that smell, from those pet shops you used to go to at the mall to look at hamsters when you were a kid. Not a memory we want reprised in our mouths. Seriously not good. This smell is caused by a compound that is brought about by different bacteria hanging out in the wine. When there is no stabilising agent (like sulphites) used there is a greater chance that these bacteria can be present in the wine. This compound can even develop after some time so it may not be there when you first drink it, popping up after a few hours or a day after opening. Regardless of how it got there, however, it's gotta be tipped.

One last thing to be wary of is volatile acidity or VA. This is an obvious one to most as it manifests as that vinegary smell and taste. VA comes about when there has been a little too much oxygen exposure. As we know, grapes have a lot of acid in them, but these are usually good, tasty acids like tartaric acid. When a wine gets an overload of oxygen though, some little bacteria get to work. These are known as acetic acid bacteria as that is the acid they form; the same acid that is in vinegar. This is going to start happening after a little while anyway, hence why wine left open for a few days is undrinkable. But it can come about during the winemaking process (this is another thing that sulphites protect against) or due to failure of the bottle's closure, be it cork or cap. Either way though, it's probably time to chuck it. Or even better, put it in a fermenting container and start your own mother of vinegar to ferment all your leftover wine. Gotta love that balsamic!

Now, equipped with tips and what not to sip, go forth all ye and swig to your heart's content. Cheers to you and cheers to all of us. Cheers to everything that has come about so wondrously on this earth to allow us to have something so incredible with which to toast.

Cheers!

THE END (THAT IS REALLY JUST THE BEGINNING AGAIN)

Iberia never ceases to amaze me. The land is drenched in tradition and culture that I hope as time goes on will only continue to be unearthed and revived. The beating heart of this place is strong, so who knows what stories it has yet to share. We just happen to be alive at a very opportune time in which we are able to see it. Gone are the uncompromising days where the true beauty of this place is smothered by overly sharp acidities and lashings of oak; now it is time for the real face of Iberia to see the light. And to shine!

The future, I trust, will be ripe with indigenous varieties that grow in deep understanding of the earth, carefully shaped by the gentlest of human hands with the intention of producing vinous delights steeped in local tradition, which pour from the land onto the tongue, conveying all the secrets and truths that run back to the beginning of time. I will be awaiting this longed-for future with bated breath, my hand trembling in excitement as it grips the stem of my glass that stretches out to catch every one of those delicious drops. I hope you'll share in my enthusiasm, if not my bottle.

I thank you for joining me on this latest trip. I look forward to taking more together soon. Because the quest for bomb vinho is one that will never have an end. There will forever be exceptions that defy the rules and there will always be new things to be discovered. Be happy that there is no conclusion or destination so that we may forever enjoy the ongoing ride.

I am pleased, throughout all of these experiences, to have learnt that there is actually no singular answer to this question of "What makes a wine 'good'?" There is instead a plethora of answers, in a jungle's worth of variations, and every person will have different reasons for what makes a wine special to them. Next time you feel small and lacking in wine knowledge, know that not everyone knows everything (in fact, no one does) and that nothing can definitively be The Best. Most of those people are probably only saying that it's the best cause someone told them to think that and they've most likely done little field research to discover their own reasoning.

So fuck them and trip and sip your way to your own bomb vinho!

That's what I plan to do. And there's a long road ahead. As I write this final chapter, I sit on the island of Hydra, a place awash in the seas of Greece. The wind is picking up and the skies are greying with the first rains of autumn, expected any minute now. This island, like the scores around it, like the mainland too, is ancient, built on hard stone and deep tradition. It's as if I have been pulled here by an invisible force. Something quivers, restless and ready. Or maybe that's me. This place, like the Iberian Peninsula, feels stretched taut, fit to bursting with the stories cut from the cloth of this land, all weaving together its masterpiece.

There is much to discover here and too few voices who have stood upon the soapbox to share its wonders. The wines here have been known for millennia, while the Greek wine culture was and is so influential to many others within its radius. In a number of surrounding countries, the names of popular winemaking grapes will often translate simply to "the Greek one," as these were once spread far and wide during the heights of Hellenic power, the extent of their reach clearly visible in this widespread use of Greek grape varieties (before the Ottomans took over and clamped down on all this winemaking nonsense, that is). The country still teems with unique varieties and ancient techniques that no doubt promise to delight. Challenges posed by culture, policy, and recent economics may have held Greek winemakers back from the main stage in modern times, but I sense that change is coming along with the rains. There's only one way to find out . . .

So, with that, I must say goodbye to you, but to Greece I say hello. I have a strong feeling the next time we meet I will have a lot more to share.

ACKNOWLEDGMENTS

It has been a long and difficult journey to get to this point. Yes, I have enjoyed a lot of it, but it hasn't always been a sweet ride. From language barriers to haunting bureaucracy and the occasional narcissistic tormenting boss, there have been plenty of potholes in the road.

For that reason, I want to say, from the depths of my heart, a huge thank you to all that have helped me along the way.

In particular my parents, Shaun and Hester, who since day one have always stood behind me and supported all my crazy hair-brained schemes, my brother Corby and sister Lydia who do the same and my partner Amy, who not only supports these wild ideas, but immediately starts thinking of ways to put them into motion.

A special thanks to Lara and George of Restaurant SEM for their wonderful foreword and continued support, not only by giving me a job but also a soapbox to yell about wine from (and of course, continue my learning).

In the making of this book, I want to thank Chloe Sisson for her wonderful editing, Frances Baca for her brilliant book design, Julia Blochtein for her splendid illustrations, and Holly Ovenden for her amazing cover art. You have all done such wonderful work which has polished this rock into the gem that it is!

Also, thank you to all my friends who have helped along the way, you know who you are. Either lightening the load of living in foreign countries or simply sharing a beer (or wine) when the sun is shining, it has helped a lot.

To all the winemakers that have been so generous with your knowledge and time, I also give a sincere thanks. Without you there would be nothing to fill these pages and I am forever grateful.

A special shout out should go to all you fuckers who have stood in my way thus far as well (in particular that aforementioned boss, who threatened me with never finding another job in the wine industry). Regardless of your obstructions, I did it anyway. Thanks, at least, for providing the energy to prove you wrong!

Lastly, thank you to you too, dear reader. Can't wait to share more!

Trippin' and Sippin'
Adam Lovell

ISBN 979-8988516033

Published by Parea Books
www.pareabooks.com
about@pareabooks.com

EDITORS
Chloë Sisson and Amy Snook

PROOFREADER
Janet Blake

COVER DESIGN AND ILLUSTRATION
Holly Ovenden

INTERIOR DESIGN
Frances Baca

INTERIOR ILLUSTRATIONS
Julia Blochtein

AUTHOR PHOTOGRAPHS
Amy Snook

Typeset in Mundo Serif and Timmons NY

Printed in Colombia